Grammar Mastery —for Better Writing

Teacher Guide

Curriculum Unit

Mary Louise Wanamaker

The Author

Mary Louise Wanamaker, who earned her M.A. at St. Louis University, has taught English, grades 9–12, to all ability levels. She concentrated on developing curriculum during her sixteen years as principal. Wanamaker also has twelve years' experience as a teacher supervisor at Province High Schools, Los Angeles, where she worked with principals on curriculum matters.

The Publishing Team

Rose Schaffer, M.A., President/Chief Executive Officer
Bernadette Vetter, M.A., Vice President
Diana Culbertson, Ph.D., Editor
Amy Hollis, B.S.J., Editor

Cover Design

Susan Sheaffer Curtis, B.A.

ISBN-13: 978-1-56077-628-4
ISBN-10: 1-56077-628-5

Contents

Page

Introduction iv
Teacher Notes v
Principles for Teaching the Workbooks vi
Techniques for Teaching and Drill vii

Level 1

Unit 1 Basic Patterns 1
Unit 2 Verbs 7
Unit 3 Nouns 10
Unit 4 Pronouns 14
Unit 5 Adjectives 18
Unit 6 Adverbs 21
Unit 7 Verbals 24
Final Examination 29
Workbook Answers 31
Unit Test Answers 72

Level 2

Unit 1 Basic Materials 76
Unit 2 Adverb Clauses 80
Unit 3 Adjective Clauses 84
Unit 4 Noun Clauses 87
Unit 5 Compound Sentences 91
Unit 6 Mood, Potential, Parallelism, Transitions 95
Final Examination 99
Workbook Answers 101
Unit Test Answers 127

Introduction

Can you believe that the teaching of grammar and writing can be exciting? Every day there will be new knowledge, new techniques, and new successes. And, best of all, with the workbooks, the teaching of formal grammar will be completed in two years. No more rehashing of the same ideas or the same rules year after year. Students will have the necessary grammar background to concentrate on the content of their writing without worrying about the nitty-gritty of its correctness.

This *Teacher Guide* has been designed to show how to use the information and exercises in the workbooks most effectively. It suggests various activities with strategies to reinforce the material and help plan lessons and assignments. It also includes unit tests with answers and a final examination.

Teacher Notes

This is a great time to be a teacher. Our students need us as never before. They are living in a fast-paced technological age. It is our responsibility to prepare them to face the challenges with courage, but, above all, with self-confidence. We must guide them in the development of their natural strengths and teach them to value themselves and others as they prepare to become contributing members of society.

The ability to write clear, forceful, correct prose is one of the most important skills we can teach them. To write well, however, our students need a thorough grammar background. For many years teachers have been propagandized about the evils of teaching grammar. Students are supposed to learn the use of grammar and mechanics in the course of their writing as a spontaneous discovery rather than as a structural part of the curriculum. I have long suspected that this is a case of wishful thinking.

To make grammar understandable and interesting, English teachers need a method that teaches each concept sequentially, one step at a time, always connecting each step to the complete sentence. Knowledge of all the components of the simple sentence must be taught before the study of complex structures. There must be clear explanations, many drills, and constant review. But the study of grammar is not an end; it is only a means to an end. The focus always must be on the development of writing skills. It is on this principle that the workbooks are based.

Learning is a strong motivator. When students realize that they are participants in the learning process and that they can grasp the grammatical concepts presented in a multi-sensory, structural method, teaching reaches a new dimension; it becomes exciting and meaningful. The English departments of La Reina High School, Thousand Oaks, California and St. Bonaventure High School, Ventura, California piloted the workbooks for two years, and they enthusiastically endorse their success in the classroom. I am positive you will find the books just as rewarding.

Principles for Teaching the Workbooks

1. Always read the explanations in the workbooks with the students and work through each example.
2. It is better if students do NOT write in the workbooks immediately. Use exercises more than once for drills. Have students write in the books only when you feel that they understand the materials.
3. Be consistent. Spend at least fifteen minutes a day, four days a week, using the workbooks. Knowledge needs daily review to be retained. Don't be concerned about what you think students might be missing while studying grammar. In the long run, they will be much stronger English students.
4. Emphasize the fact that grammar is an essential element in the development of effective writing skills. As much as possible, link concepts taught to the students' writing.
5. Do not teach by diagramming sentences.
6. Do not label parts of speech. Understanding comes with how a word is used in a sentence.
7. Make sure students *speak grammar.* (See Techniques for Teaching and Drill on page vii.)
8. Do not have students memorize abstract rules and definitions.
9. Keep the class alive. Use shorter drills. Get all students to participate. Nothing causes lethargy faster than a monotonous reciting of answers. Make the students proud and excited about learning.
10. Vary drill methods. (See Techniques for Teaching and Drill on page vii.)
11. Vary strategies. The main purpose of teaching is to facilitate learning. How we teach is directly related to the kind of learning desired. Many techniques can be used to facilitate learning. No one should have to sit through a long explanation on grammar, or work on extensive grammar assignments. (See Techniques for Teaching and Drill, page vii.)
12. Make use of the review provided in the workbooks.
13. Do not belabor a point. When you feel that the students seem to understand a concept, move on. Students master ideas at different times, and the concepts are often repeated throughout the workbook.
14. Frequent evaluation of students' performance is desirable. Short quizzes can be just as effective as long tests. Quizzes also indicate where the students need drill. The unit tests in the *Teacher Guide* should be used as final evaluations for each unit.
15. Don't get discouraged. Sometimes students will understand a concept, but as soon as another idea is added, they become confused. For example, they might easily understand the intransitive verb, but the introduction of the transitive verb could confuse them.
16. Integrate vocabulary words whenever possible.
17. A few of your students might not grasp the concepts you are teaching. Do not worry. This is a fact of life. Remember, these students will know more from studying grammar sequentially and with drill than from any other method.
18. Grammar is only a means to an end. Its purpose is not to make grammarians, but writers. Your students might not remember all the concepts you taught, but they will remember the essentials in developing their writing skills.

Techniques for Teaching and Drill

Group Work

1. Put students into groups of no more than four or five.
2. Group students so that there is as little movement as possible.
3. Group work should usually last about five minutes.
4. Choose a student monitor but change monitors periodically.
5. Vary strategies for correcting exercises or homework.
   a. Give the monitor the answers. Students give answers in groups. If a disagreement occurs, the monitor has the final say.
   b. Students go through the exercise. If they are not sure about an answer, the monitor marks the problem. At the end of the group work, the teacher explains the answer.
   c. A student reads the answers. (This can be part of the exercise, or the entire exercise.) If students disagree with an answer, they mark the number. The answer is clarified by either the students or the teacher.
6. Have students read original compositions in groups and critique them. The best composition from each group can be read to the entire class.
7. Use groups for cooperative learning. This is excellent for review. The teacher gives each group a paper with review questions or sentences. Students work out the answers together. The teacher reads the answers and the group evaluates its performance.

Blackboard or Overhead Projector

1. Use the blackboard or overhead projector frequently.
2. Have students put their work on the blackboard as soon as they come to class.
3. Have three or four sentences on the blackboard each class period to clarify errors, to teach a specific point, or to drill.
4. Have exercises for drill on transparencies. These can be used many times.
5. Students should learn to *speak grammar.* Speaking grammar means that the student gives not only the answer, but all the facts in the sentence that have already been taught.

Example

Teacher: Name the kinds of verbs in the sentence:

1. Emilio hit a homerun yesterday afternoon.

Student: The verb *hit* is transitive. Its complement is *homerun.* The basic pattern is *Emilio hit homerun.* The subject is *Emilio* (doer). The modifiers of the verb are *yesterday* and *afternoon,* both answering the question *when.*

Speaking grammar reinforces concepts.

Vocabulary Department

Teachers must never lose sight of vocabulary development. Good writing needs a strong vocabulary. Integrate as much as possible by using current vocabulary in original sentences. Have students keep a journal of new words from their reading; giving the word, the definition, the sentence in which they found the word, and an original sentence. Check these journals periodically.

Level 1

Unit 1

Basic Patterns

Objective

- To understand the three basic sentence patterns and their importance in writing

Subject and Predicate

Pages 1–3; Exercises 1–2

Spend only two or three lessons on subject and predicate. There will be constant review during the study of basic patterns.

Students should learn to *speak grammar* when giving answers. As each concept is taught, have them use the correct terms.

Work quietly in your room tonight.

Student: The subject *you* is understood. The predicate is *work*.

Stress the "doer" in a sentence. Introduce subject with phrases so students know that the phrase can never be the subject. This is important, especially when students study subject-verb agreement.

A *pot* of soup boils on the stove.
A *shelf* of books fell to the floor.

First Basic Pattern

Pages 4–7; Exercises 3–7

Demonstrate basic pattern on the board. The basic patterns are

1. subject, intransitive verb
2. subject, transitive verb, complement
3. subject, linking verb, subject complement

It is very important that students understand each basic pattern as it is taught. Drill often and have students write original sentences.

In the first basic pattern, the verb is intransitive; it stands alone. Nothing completes its meaning, and the subject is always the "doer". Use **Exercises 3–7** to drill this concept. Vary your methods of drill. (See Techniques for Teaching and Drill on page vii.)

Teach modifiers so that students understand a modifier is never a part of the basic pattern. When modifying verbs, modifiers answer the questions how, when, where, why, or how much (to what extent). Ask the students to state the question the modifier answers. **Exercises 1** and **2** can also be used to drill modifiers.

Many exercises in the book can be used for homework assignments. As a rule, it is better for students to use notebook paper rather than to write in the workbooks. After they understand the material, the final writing in the workbooks reinforces what they have learned.

Speaking grammar also helps to reinforce the material.

The children played on the swings.

Student: The basic pattern is *children played*. The subject is *children*, and the verb is intransitive. The modifier, *on the swings*, answers *where*.

Mini-Drill Suggestions

1. Have each student write a sentence using an intransitive verb with no modifiers. Choose some students to put their sentences on the blackboard. Then ask them to add two modifiers. Correct the sentences with the class. This drill could also be done in small groups.
2. Dramatize sentences by giving a student a paper with a command, such as "Walk to the front of the room." Have the class state the basic pattern: *John walked.*
3. Read the following ten sentences aloud. Ask students to raise their hands if the verb is NOT intransitive. Ask students to make it intransitive.
    1. Mary left in a hurry.
    2. She swims every morning.
    3. Bob ate his lunch in the cafeteria. (*Bob ate in the cafeteria.*)
    4. Judy walked quickly to her seat.
    5. Jerry played drums in the band. (*Jerry played in the band.*)
    6. Jean cried during the movie.
    7. Tom works at Pizza Hut.
    8. Gloria sang with her sister.
    9. Sydney writes well.
    10. Alice giggled during the talk.

Optional Assignment

Instruct students to find four or five good sentences using intransitive verbs from a story or novel they are reading. The sentences do not have to come from the same paragraph. Have them give the title and the author of the work and underline the intransitive verbs. This assignment makes students aware of good sentence structure.

Second Basic Pattern

Pages 7–23; Exercises 8–25

It is important that students understand the concept *transitive*. A transitive verb always has a noun or pronoun that completes its meaning and answers the questions what or whom. Use both *complement* and *direct object* for the word that completes the transitive verb.

Read page 7 of Workbook 1 with the class. This page includes a comparison showing the same verb as intransitive and transitive.

Have students speak grammar.

My brother wrote an essay last night.

Student: The basic pattern is *brother wrote essay*. The subject doer is *brother*. The verb is transitive. The complement is *essay*. The modifiers are *last night*.

Exercise 11 is an original essay by a student. Have students explain why the verbs are transitive or intransitive. Instruct them to imitate this essay in a paragraph about an experience they have had. Have them read their paragraphs in small groups and put the best one on the overhead.

Challenge students to master **Exercise 12.** Passive voice is taught in this section because only transitive verbs speak both actively and passively. In the passive voice, the complement (receiver) is in the subject position, and the doer is either the object of the preposition *by* or eliminated. Intransitive verbs have no receiver, so they always speak actively. Demonstrate this on the board: John broke dish. Dish was broken (by John).

For a quick drill, give a sentence and have students change the verb to the passive or vice versa.

I wrote letter. *Letter was written.*

The fence was painted. *John painted the fence.*

Exercise 24 is a difficult assignment. It is best to go over it orally with the students and then have them write the answers out for homework.

Optional Assignment

Instruct students to write out four or five sentences from a story or novel. Have them give the title and the author (for example, *The Jilting of Granny Weatherall* by Katherine Anne Porter).

Third Basic Pattern

Pages 24–32; Exercises 26–36

The concept of linking verbs is often difficult for students. A linking verb does not act. It is a state-of-being verb. Demonstrate on the board before working in the book.

Bob became a doctor.

Bob cannot become. *Doctor* and *Bob* are the same. *Doctor* complements *Bob.*

My father looked very angry. (linking)

She looked at the pictures. (intransitive)

The tennis player grew tired. (linking)

I grew flowers in my garden. (transitive)

Review the sentences on pages 24 and 25 of the workbook for further practice with distinguishing between linking and transitive verbs.

Students often confuse subject complement and verb complement. Explain that a verb complement completes the *verb.* It can be a noun or a pronoun.

Bill plays football.

The complement completes *plays.*

A subject complement completes the *subject.* It can be a noun, pronoun, or adjective. Note: The subject complement is sometimes called the predicate nominative or predicate adjective.

Mr. Jones is an engineer.

Engineer complements the subject, telling who Mr. Jones is. When an adjective complements the subject, it is a complement, not a modifier.

Passive voice and linking verbs are confusing because they both use a form of *be*. If a noun, pronoun, or adjective follows the form of *be*, the verb is linking.

was captain   *is* cheerleader   *could be* successful.

If the third principal part of the verb follows forms of the verb *be*, the verb is passive.

was *stolen*   is *taken*   could be *seen*.

This concept will be repeated in Unit 2.

Put the following sentences on a transparency or on the board to drill linking verbs and passive voice. Go over these examples with the students.

1. John is a good soccer player. (*linking*)
2. Joe's arm could have been cut during the game. (*passive voice*)
3. Jerry must be tired after the marathon. (*linking*)
4. Bob could be a good student. (*linking*)
5. The movie had been seen three times. (*passive voice*)
6. The books were taken to the library. (*passive voice*)
7. She must be unhappy about the outcome. (*linking*)
8. He will be captain of the volleyball team next year. (*linking*)
9. Sheila could be a great artist. (*linking*)
10. Brian's talk was very persuasive. (*linking*)
11. Betty was injured in the game. (*passive voice*)
12. My room was painted last week. (*passive voice*)
13. My room is a light green. (*linking*)
14. The argument was settled peacefully. (*passive voice*)
15. The debate was very competitive. (*linking*)
16. The debate was held in the auditorium. (*passive voice*)
17. Our math exam was extremely difficult. (*linking*)
18. The exam will be taken in the gym. (*passive voice*)
19. Keith must be a good actor. (*linking*)
20. Jean should be taken to the hospital. (*passive voice*)

Test

Level 1—Unit 1

Basic Patterns

Unit 1 completes the material for the first quarter.

Test

Level 1—Unit 1

Basic Patterns

Name ______________________

Date ______________________

Directions: Write *INT* (intransitive), *TR* (transitive), or *L* (linking) for each verb.

___ 1. The two secretaries work in the old office.

___ 2. Many students enjoy football and baseball.

___ 3. Basketball is becoming a very popular sport.

___ 4. The new accountant made two serious mistakes.

___ 5. Her pies always taste delicious.

___ 6. Bob is a real winner.

___ 7. We all joined in the fun.

___ 8. None of the work was finished on time.

___ 9. The mail was distributed late today.

___ 10. Her purse was stolen from her car.

___ 11. My little sister hates spinach.

___ 12. Where did you put my book?

___ 13. My mother went to the doctor yesterday.

___ 14. The team was optimistic about the outcome.

___ 15. Prudence is a virtue.

___ 16. Across the bridge stood the entire basketball team.

___ 17. Bring the package to me.

___ 18. She laid her pencil on the desk.

___ 19. The music sounds beautiful.

___ 20. We read *A Tale of Two Cities* in class.

___ 21. The plot of the story is very interesting.

___ 22. Have you ever read *The Red Pony* by John Steinbeck?

___ 23. It is an excellent novel.

___ 24. Young pine trees grow very fast.

___ 25. Winter seems remote during the summer.

___ 26. Jean hastened to her algebra class.

___ 27. The long days of summer are enjoyable.

___ 28. We will go to Australia next month.

___ 29. Read the article carefully.

___ 30. This door leads to my classroom.

___ 31. I taught there for ten years.

___ 32. Miss Jones is an excellent math teacher.

___ 33. My ruler is broken.

___ 34. Regular exercises build muscles.

___ 35. Tom rides his bicycle to work every day.

___ 36. Janice sold her typewriter and bought a computer.

___ 37. We flew to Alaska last week.

___ 38. The sunset last night was truly beautiful.

___ 39. It appeared red on the picture.

___ 40. Did you read the paper this morning?

___ 41. I met the president of that company this morning.

___ 42. He is a very important man.

___ 43. Pictures were taken of his latest projects.

___ 44. The pictures were clear.

___ 45. Joe's kitten stretched out at the foot of his bed.

___ 46. The package was mailed yesterday afternoon.

___ 47. I enjoy algebra and history.

___ 48. Bob is an exceptional basketball player.

___ 49. Whom did you meet at the party?

___ 50. We thoroughly enjoyed the outing.

Unit 2

Verbs

Objective

Pages 33–51; Exercises 37–51

- To acquire a background on verbs and their importance in writing

This unit should not take more than three weeks. You can always refer to it when necessary.

Review the principal parts of the verb, especially the irregular verbs and the tenses they build. Study thoroughly the irregular verb *am, was, been.*

Teach the future perfect tense but do not dwell on it, as it is used very infrequently.

Students studied linking verbs and passive voice in Unit 1, so the progressive form will not be too difficult to teach. The explanation and the exercises should be adequate.

Because linking verbs, passive voice, and the progressive form of the verb use forms of the verb *be*, the conjugations on pages 37 and 38 of the workbook should prove helpful. **Exercise 44** can be used as a test.

The purpose for the study of tense is to make students aware that in their writing, verb tenses must be consistent. **Exercise 46** shows how inconsistency weakens an essay.

Troublesome Verbs

Troublesome verbs need much drill, especially *lie, lay, lain* (transitive) and *lay, laid, laid* (intransitive). The chief difficulty is that *lay* is the past tense for *lie,* **lay,** *lain* and the present tense for **lay,** *laid, laid.* The suffix *-ing* can be added only to the present tense: *lying* for the intransitive verb and *laying* for the transitive verb. Quick drills each day will help students with this difficulty.

> I laid the pencil on the table. Now the pencil *is lying* on the table.
>
> He lies on the couch. Now he *is lying* on the couch.

Exercise 50 should help them understand these verbs. Do this exercise several times.

The **Review Test on Verbs** is an excellent tool to evaluate students' knowledge of verbs.

Test

Level 1—Unit 2

Verbs

Test

Level 1—Unit 2

Verbs

Name ____________________

Date ____________________

Part A.

Directions: Give the tense of the following verbs.

1. worked __________
2. had found __________
3. will send __________
4. took __________
5. was given __________
6. were stolen __________
7. has flown __________
8. bought __________
9. did leave __________
10. have believed __________
11. had seen __________
12. will go __________
13. have taken __________
14. will have gone __________
15. is leaving __________
16. will send __________
17. had torn __________
18. will buy __________
19. does want __________
20. are __________

Part B.

Directions: Change the verbs from passive voice to active voice without changing tense.

21. had been found ____________________
22. will be sung ____________________
23. is given ____________________
24. was chosen ____________________
25. has been lost ____________________
26. will be taken ____________________
27. has been accepted ____________________
28. was finished ____________________
29. were taken ____________________
30. was torn ____________________

Part C.

Directions: Write each verb in the given tense.

31. John (write) several letters to his friends. (past) ____________
32. She (play) softball or Little League. (present) ____________
33. The class (laugh) at the joke. (past) ____________
34. The boy (break) the dish in the cafeteria. (past perfect) ____________
35. She (tear) her sweater. (present perfect) ____________
36. The team probably (lose) the game. (future) ____________
37. John (bring) the package for his mother. (past) ____________
38. My little brother (eat) the entire pie. (past perfect) ____________
39. He (leave) the room. (past) ____________
40. We (see) the movie next Sunday. (future) ____________

Part D.

Directions: Write *INT* for intransitive, *TR* for transitive, or *L* for linking for each verb.

___ 41. We all assembled in the auditorium.

___ 42. Her essay was destroyed by the fire.

___ 43. Her coat is very expensive.

___ 44. The student was very dejected.

___ 45. His main idea was not accepted by the committee.

___ 46. He brought the matter before the jury.

___ 47. She has chosen the material for her dress.

___ 48. The team practiced all day Friday.

___ 49. Everyone cheered the team to victory.

___ 50. Keith is a natural artist.

Unit 3

Nouns

Objective

Pages 56–89; Exercises 52–80

- To understand all the components of nouns, their uses, and relationships

Most students understand person, gender, and number of nouns from elementary school, so this section should not take too much time.

Case

Nouns in many languages change form when they are used differently. A noun in the nominative case would have a different ending from a noun in the objective case. Nouns that have different endings are called *inflected.* When nouns do not change forms, they are called *noninflected.* Our nouns are noninflected; they do not change when used differently in a sentence. Because this is true, the number of words that rhyme in our language is very limited. Write the word *love* on the board. Ask students to give words that rhyme (*shove, dove, above*). Do this exercise with other words, for example, *friend* (*end, send, fend, rend*) . When languages are inflected, it is easier to find rhymes.

Before studying the explanation in the book, write the following sentence on the board.

Shirley, a good volleyball player, received a college scholarship.

Ask a student to underline all the nouns in this sentence. Ask the class, from your study of Unit 1, does each noun have the same use in this sentence? How is *Shirley* used? (*Subject*) Is *player* used the same way? (No) They are the same person, but their use in the sentence is different. What about *scholarship*? *college*?

This sentence shows that nouns are used differently, but they do not change their form. The nouns are noninflected. The way a noun is used in a sentence is called *case.* Nouns have different cases because they have different uses.

Students should have little difficulty with the nominative case. Start objective case as soon as you think the students understand nominative case. Case is reviewed during the study of pronouns.

Drill troublesome prepositions, especially *angry at a thing/with a person, different from,* and *need of* using **Exercises 60–65.**

For **Exercise 64, part B,** have students read their original paragraphs in groups. Put the best ones on the overhead.

Poems can also be used to teach grammar. The poem "Fog" by Carl Sandburg is a good example. Write the poem on a transparency. Have students find the prepositional phrases. Note: The last *on* is not a preposition. Why? Ask students how these phrases add to the meaning of the poem. Briefly discuss the content of the poem.

Possessive case is explained thoroughly in the workbook. Do the exercises orally and in small groups. **Exercise 66** is effective as an oral drill.

Capitalization of Nouns

Teach a few rules at a time and review often using **Exercises 70–73**.

The study of subject-verb agreement is very important and requires frequent drills. **Exercises 74–80** reinforce each set of rules, but the difficulty for students is remembering. Using transparencies frequently is the best way to drill this material.

Mini-Drill Suggestions

1. To drill material already studied, put about four sentences with errors to correct on the board each day.
2. Have students write four or five sentences with errors and read them to the class. Instruct the class to correct the errors.
3. Have a student-taught lesson. Students should turn in their lesson plans for approval a day or two before the lesson. With special certificates or rewards for teaching a good lesson, students will be more willing to volunteer.

   Student: Today I am going to teach possessive case. Possessive case shows ownership. For a noun to show ownership, the apostrophe is used. If a plural noun ends in *s*, add an apostrophe. If a noun does not end in *s*, add an apostrophe *s*. (Demonstrate on board.) For joint ownership, the last person receives the apostrophe. For separate ownership, each is given the apostrophe.

   Look at the following words. Where would you put the apostrophe? (The student could have these words on the board before class.)

window	children	day
fence	desks	hour
computer	sheep	Tom and Joe bookstore (joint ownership)
ladies	mice	Peter and Mike cars were in the race.
child	enemy	

   Short Quiz: The student-teacher passes out papers with the following sentences. Quizzes could be student-teacher or class corrected.

   1. I left John book on the counter.
   2. The boy record is very good.
   3. Men hats are for sale.
   4. The teacher report was accurate.
   5. The woman reply came too late.
   6. I sent Mary article to the paper.
   7. Jim bought two dollar worth of candy.
   8. Alice and Lisa bicycles were in the back of the room.
   9. We plan to go on a week vacation.
   10. Ted and Laura house is up for sale.

Test

Level 1—Unit 3
Nouns
This unit should complete the material for the second quarter.

Name ____________________

Date ____________________

Test
Level 1—Unit 3
Nouns

Part A.

Directions: For each italicized word , write *N* for nominative case subject, *DO* for direct object, *IO* for indirect object, *SC* for subject complement (predicative nominative), or *OP* for object of the preposition.

During the *war* my brother was injured.
1

Twilight comes between *daylight* and *darkness*.
2 3 4

The cause of his *failures* was bad *habits*.
5 6

The horror movie gave my *brother* *nightmares*.
7 8

The class sent *Bob* a *bouquet* of flowers.
9 10

The store across the *street* remains *open* on *Sundays*.
11 12 13

Tom and *Jim* gave an *excuse* for their *absence*.
14 15 16 17

Judy has been *captain* of the volleyball *squad* for two *years*.
18 19 20

Outside the *room* Sylvia met with a little *adventure*.
21 22

Under the immense reading *glass* in the *cartoon* were
23 24
villainous-looking *characters*.
25

1. __________
2. __________
3. __________
4. __________
5. __________
6. __________
7. __________
8. __________
9. __________
10. __________
11. __________
12. __________
13. __________
14. __________
15. __________
16. __________
17. __________
18. __________
19. __________
20. __________
21. __________
22. __________
23. __________
24. __________
25. __________

Part B.

Directions: Write the letter of the correct answer.

___ 26. The jelly in these sandwiches (A. taste B. tastes) good.

___ 27. A shelf of books (A. was B. were) in her bedroom.

___ 28. The trees in our backyard (A. have B. has) many bird nests.

___ 29. The twins, as well as their sister, (A. attend B. attends) Washington High School.

___ 30. The safe with its contents (A. was B. were) damaged by the fire.

___ 31. A bunch of grapes (A. was B. were) in the basket.

___ 32. Two-thirds of the questions (A. was B. were) very difficult.

___ 33. A number of my friends (A. agrees B. agree) with me.

___ 34. The team (A. is B. are) leaving for the game at 2:00 P.M.

___ 35. The number of incorrect answers (A. annoys B. annoy) the teacher.

___ 36. Economics (A. is B. are) required for graduation.

___ 37. About half of the players (A. plans B. plan) to go to camp.

___ 38. Mathematics (A. is B. are) required for two years.

___ 39. A number of boys (A. expects B. expect) to receive an A.

___ 40. Twelve books (A. was B. were) lying on the desk.

Part C.

Directions: Write *C* if the words in each sentence are capitalized correctly; otherwise, write *I*.

___ 41. We met Ex-Governor Brown at the leadership convention in New York.

___ 42. We visited the President of the Kodak Company.

___ 43. When you travel west in the morning, you will not have the sun in your eyes.

___ 44. We are planning a barbecue on Labor Day.

___ 45. The President of the United States will visit Los Angeles in the near future.

___ 46. The freshman class of Liberty High School will elect their chairperson next week.

___ 47. Professor Jones, Professor of history, is a well-known historian.

___ 48. My parents want to visit the south in autumn.

___ 49. My mother is planning to return to college in the fall.

___ 50. My father once met the president of the United States.

Unit 4

Pronouns

Objective

Pages 90–111; Exercises 81–101

- To acquire a thorough background in the kinds of pronouns and their uses

Be sure students understand the meaning of *antecedent.*

There are many kinds of pronouns, but the most important are the personal and the indefinite pronouns.

Because pronouns take the place of nouns, they have the same cases as nouns. Unlike nouns, pronouns are inflected; there are different pronouns for each case.

Pronouns and Case

Nominative Case

Have students memorize the nominative case pronouns. Emphasize that nominative case pronouns always follow a linking verb.

Jack is he.

Jack is nominative case, subject; *he* is nominative case, subject complement.

Give short drills until this concept is mastered. Write the following on the board and have students state as many pronouns as possible for each sentence.

1. The best athlete was ______.
2. The culprit could have been ____.
3. The winners were______ .
4. It was ____ .
5. The ringleader is _____ .
6. The musicians were ______.
7. The scientists were______ .
8. The greatest gymnast was ______.
9. My best friend is _____ .
10. His teammates were______.

The subject complement pronoun must agree with its antecedent in gender and number.

Objective Case

Have students memorize objective case pronouns. Work through **Exercises 84–88** drilling objective case.

Possessive Case

Have students memorize the possessive case pronouns. Demonstrate using nouns and pronouns in the possessive case. Put the following sentences on the board:

That was Jack's hat. That was his hat.

It was Mary's coat. It was her coat.

Possessive case pronouns can also be used as modifiers. Work through **Exercise 89** with the class.

Demonstrative Pronouns

These and compound personal pronouns are easily understood and need little drill.

Indefinite Pronouns

It is important for students to memorize indefinite pronouns because some are singular, some are plural, and some can be either singular or plural.

Some indefinite pronouns use the apostrophe to show ownership.

> It was anyone's game.
> Mary was everybody's favorite.
> One's desires cannot always be fulfilled.

Never use the apostrophe with personal pronouns to show ownership.

At this time, review apostrophes with contractions. The apostrophe in a contraction takes the place of the missing letter: are not–aren't; did not–didn't; it is–it's. Although students probably were taught this in grade school, they often confuse *it's* (contraction, meaning *it is*) and *its* (ownership).

Correlatives

Be sure that students know that correlatives must be used in pairs. *Neither . . . nor* should never be written *neither . . . or.*

Agreement of Pronouns with Their Antecedents

In **Exercise 99**, students could also underline the antecedents.

Drill subject-verb agreement often. Use **Exercises 100–101**. Have transparencies for daily drill. It might be wise to review singular and plural nouns at this time, especially such nouns as *the number, a number,* and *gymnastics.*

Mini-Drill Suggestions

Use mini-drill suggestions for nouns on page 11.

Test

Level 1—Unit 4

Pronouns

Test
Level 1—Unit 4
Pronouns

Name ____________________

Date ____________________

Directions: Write the letter of the correct answer.

___ 1. The majority of voters showed (A. its B. their) disagreement violently.

___ 2. The assembly voted on (A. its B. their) grievances.

___ 3. Each of the presents in the basket belongs to (A. he B. him).

___ 4. Everyone in the class must write (A. his, her B. their) own research paper.

___ 5. Each of us gave (A. his, her B. their) opinion.

___ 6. Neither Tom nor his sister wants (A. they B. them) to leave.

___ 7. My two cousins, Bob and (A. he B. him), will be visiting us this summer.

___ 8. (A. It's B. Its) use in the study of medicine is important.

___ 9. At the assembly, the principal gave the highest scholarship to Sam and (A. her B. she).

___ 10. He had only praise for Grace and (A. I B. me).

___ 11. Let's you and (A. I B. me) go to the concert.

___ 12. (A. Who B. Whom) did you see yesterday in the library?

___ 13. The teacher told (A. we B. us) all about the problem.

___ 14. To (A. who B. whom) was she speaking?

___ 15. (A. We B. Us) are going to the game tomorrow night.

___ 16. My best friends are Jerry and (A. she B. her).

___ 17. It would have to be (A. he B. him) in the show.

___ 18. The coach gave Jack and (A. he B. him) special awards.

___ 19. Our win against Compton was due to Jack and (A. he B. him).

___ 20. (A. Who B. Whom) are you photographing?

___ 21. Give (A. she B. her) all the help possible.

___ 22. The teacher corrected the mistake (A. himself, herself B. hisself).

___ 23. Every one of the books has (A. their B. its) cover torn.

___ 24. (A. Whoever B. Whomever) fails the test will fail the class.

___ 25. A good skater must practice (A. his, her B. their) routine daily.

___ 26. The most skillful player was (A. he B. him).

___ 27. Mother bought my sister and (A. I B. me) new dresses.

___ 28. Jeff shared his lunch with Molly and (A. I B. me).

___ 29. This softball is (A. hers B. her's).

___ 30. Mary and (A. she B. her) left the dance early.

___ 31. Everyone saw (A. they B. them) at the game.

___ 32. Several boys compared their grades with (A. ours B. our's).

___ 33. Please give (A. we B. us) the report as soon as possible.

___ 34. Send (A. her B. she) my picture.

___ 35. The best player is certainly (A. her B. she).

___ 36. Did you see (A. he B. him) at the show?

___ 37. To (A. who B. whom) did you send the letter?

___ 38. The better player could be (A. she B. her).

___ 39. Bob and (A. he B. him) are going on vacation.

___ 40. The winner must be (A. he B. him).

___ 41. Give Tom and (A. he B. him) this note.

___ 42. I gave the money to Jill and (A. she B. her)

___ 43. The better players were Brian and (A. he B. him).

___ 44. Nothing in the room made (A. he B. him) happy.

___ 45. Not one of the books (A. have B. has) any relevant material.

___ 46. She did it (A. herself B. himself).

___ 47. I agreed with Tom and (A. they B. them) on that issue.

___ 48. She gave (A. we B. us) the report.

___ 49. Jack and (A. he B. him) are planning the dance.

___ 50. To the two boys, Kevin and (A. he B. him), belong the medals.

Unit 5

Adjectives

Objective

- To understand adjectives and their comparisons

Pages 112–119; Exercises 102–108

Adjectives are not too difficult. Study two or three weeks at the most.

Emphasize with students that adjectives as a rule are modifiers that describe nouns.

Write on the blackboard the word *automobile.* Ask students for a word that would describe automobile: *red.* The red car eliminates all colors. *Saturn.* Saturn is the make of the car. This eliminates all other makes. Every time you add an adjective you eliminate other possibilities. All adjectives limit nouns. Some adjectives are called limiting to differentiate them from descriptive adjectives.

Ask students to put parentheses around the nouns in **Exercise 102.** Then ask them to give the adjective that modifies each noun.

Review the rules for capitalization of proper nouns. Do **Exercise 103** orally in class.

Review predicate adjectives. Be sure that the students understand the difference between modifiers and complements.

Comparison with Adjectives

This is important for correct usage. Drill using **Exercises 105–108.**

Balanced Comparisons

When working with comparison of adjectives, students should check to make sure that the things being compared are balanced. The sentences should compare only items of a similar kind.

It is not necessary for students to memorize the names of adjectives. It is sufficient if they recognize adjectives and use them correctly.

Optional Assignment

Have students find a paragraph from their reading that uses good adjectives.

Test

Level 1—Unit 5
Adjectives
The study of adjectives completes the work for the third quarter.

Test

Level 1—Unit 5

Adjectives

Name ______________________

Date______________________

Part A.

Directions: For the italicized adjective, write *P* for positive, *C* for comparative, or *S* for superlative.

___ 1. Who is the *brightest* girl in your math class?

___ 2. Bob is *bigger* than Tom.

___ 3. This is the *warmest* day of the year.

___ 4. Who is *healthier,* John or Peter?

___ 5. It was the *saddest* day of my life!

___ 6. Jim is *braver* than I.

___ 7. He was the *most wonderful* boy I had ever met.

___ 8. I had a *sore* throat all week.

___ 9. It is the *largest* parade I have ever seen.

___ 10. This essay is *better* than the one you turned in yesterday.

Part B.

Directions: Write the letter of the correct form.

___ 11. Who did the (A. better B. best) job, Keith or Jane?

___ 12. Tom had (A. least B. less) money than I.

___ 13. Jill is the (A. smaller B. smallest) girl on the team.

___ 14. We are (A. most talented B. more talented) than they are.

___ 15. What is the (A. shorter B. shortest) day of the year?

___ 16. I am feeling (A. well B. better) than I did yesterday.

___ 17. Jill is the (A. younger B. youngest) of her three sisters.

___ 18. Mike is the (A. busier B. busiest) of all my friends.

___ 19. Tina is the (A. luckier B. luckiest) girl I have ever met.

___ 20. My brother is (A. more successful B. most successful) than I am.

Part C.

Directions: Write *M* if the italicized word is a modifier, *C* if it is a complement.

___ 21. The haunted house had been *empty* all year.

___ 22. The ride down the river was *dangerous.*

___ 23. I met my *best* friend at the library.

___ 24. It was a bitterly *cold* day.

___ 25. Our drama teacher is generally very *humorous.*

___ 26. My little sister has a *beautiful* bike.

___ 27. It was a *lucky* break for me.

___ 28. I am generally very *lucky.*

___ 29. I had a *comfortable* bed in a cozy room.

___ 30. This rocking chair is so *comfortable.*

Unit 6

Adverbs

Objective

- To understand the uses of adverbs and their comparison

Pages 120–131;
Exercises 109–121

The study of adverbs is not too difficult. Students studied adverb modifiers of verbs in Unit 1, but adverbs can also modify adjectives and other adverbs. The explanations and **Exercises 110** and **111** should be sufficient for drill.

Students sometimes confuse adverbs and adjectives. Discuss the explanation in the workbook and work **Exercise 112** with the class orally. **Exercise 113** can be used as a homework assignment.

Comparisons with Adverbs

Since the comparison of adverbs is similar to the comparison of adjectives, this concept needs little drill. The words that cause trouble are *bad* and *badly*, *good* and *well*. Discuss the workbook explanations. Note the exception for *healthy*.

Double Negatives

As a rule, students understand that they should not use double negatives in writing. A quick review should suffice.

Many students have never heard of expletives. Discuss the explanation in the workbook. Explain that an expletive is not an adverb. It is often called a "dummy subject" because it is placed first in the sentence, but it can never be the subject.

There are five boys on the team.

In this sentence *there* is an expletive. Why?

There go the boys.

There is an adverb. Why?

Some/Somewhat

Students often confuse these words. Emphasize that *some* is always an adjective: some money, some jewelry, some papers, some work. *Somewhat* is an adverb: He was somewhat tired of listening.

For drill, give students a sentence and ask them to add an adverb.

1. The teacher was angry.
2. John was happy.
3. Everyone was delighted with the team's effort.
4. The coach spoke harshly.
5. Jane was bashful.

Optional Assignment

Have students find four or five sentences or a short paragraph from a story or novel; for example, *In Another Country* by Ernest Hemingway.

Test

Level 1—Unit 6
Adverbs

Test
Level 1—Unit 6
Adverbs

Name ____________________
Date____________________

Part A.

Directions: If the italicized word is an adverb, write *ADV*; if it is an adjective, write *ADJ*.

___ 1. John told the *funniest* joke yesterday.

___ 2. My brother plays the saxophone *well*.

___ 3. Everyone enjoys a *good* laugh.

___ 4. She *hardly* reached my knees.

___ 5. My old Chevrolet runs *surprisingly* fast.

___ 6. My English teacher spoke *eloquently* at the banquet.

___ 7. He is always *too* slow.

___ 8. I left *some* money in my room.

___ 9. I was *somewhat* afraid to enter the hall.

___ 10. We all got up *early* this morning.

Part B.

Directions: Write the letter of the correct word.

___ 11. You can (A. sure B. surely) be proud of your achievements.

___ 12. Bob plays the guitar very (A. well B. good).

___ 13. The team played (A. bad B. badly) in the tournament.

___ 14. He looked (A. awkward B. awkwardly) around the room.

___ 15. He looks (A. worried B. worriedly).

___ 16. My mother was (A. real B. really) excited this morning.

___ 17. The music sounds (A. sweet B. sweetly).

___ 18. After the accident, she rested (A. quiet B. quietly) in her room.

___ 19. We were (A. real B. really) worried about her.

___ 20. It was a (A. real B. really) experience.

___ 21. Of all the applicants, Ann is the (A. less B. least) qualified.

___ 22. I was feeling (A. bad B. badly) all morning.

___ 23. It was certainly a (A. bad B. badly) ordeal.

___ 24. This violin is truly one of the (A. better B. best) of the lot.

___ 25. My room is peaceful and (A. quiet B. quietly).

Unit 7

Verbals

Objective

- To understand the three kinds of verbals, their uses, and their importance

Pages 132–158;
Exercises 122–149

Gerunds

Before starting gerunds, be sure that students understand the meaning of *verbal.* A verbal is derived from a verb.

Ask students: What does this mean? Can a verbal be derived from *school?* Can a verbal be derived from *show*? Give a few words from which verbals can be derived.

The first verbals studied are called *gerunds*. The complement of a gerund and modifiers are called *gerund phrases.*

Washing my clothes is a real chore.

Clothes is a complement of the gerund. The basic pattern is *washing clothes is chore*

Uses of Gerunds

Because a gerund is used like a noun, it has case. Because students should have a grasp of case, do not stay too long on this material.

Students often confuse the progressive form of the verb with a gerund. **Exercise 127** should help them understand the difference.

The main gerund rule is that a singular noun or pronoun modifying a gerund must be in the *possessive case*: Tom's leaving, my moving. **Exercises 129** and **130** can also be used to test students' understanding.

Participles

A participle is a verbal adjective. Discuss the properties of a verb and of an adjective.

To explain, write a verbal on the board: working. Ask students to state nouns that *working* could modify: class working, mother working. Write a sentence using *working* as a participle: Mother, working in the kitchen, hurt her arm. Have students write two or three sentences on the board using participles.

Participles have tense and voice. The three most important tenses are present, past passive, and future active. Write the principal parts of a verb on the board: write, wrote, written. Ask students to write a sentence using *written.* You want them to understand that the third principal part, when used alone, is always a participle.

Distinguishing between Gerunds and Participles

The present tense participle, like a gerund, always adds *-ing* to the present tense. **Exercise 133** will help students understand the difference.

Dangling participles can be a fun topic. Students enjoy doing **Exercise 135.** Note for students that mistakes are often made in writing papers. For example, it is easy to start with a participle and then use the wrong noun to modify it.

Ask them to write several sentences using dangling participles. Correct them as a class.

Restrictive and Non-restrictive Participial Phrases

This is a very difficult concept. Read the explanation from the book with the class. Ask the students to indicate which nouns in **Exercise 138** are restrictive. When students have a fair idea of a restrictive noun, write a sentence on the board using a restrictive noun.

Mr. Smith, driving to school, had a slight accident.

Ask students, do you know who is driving? *(Yes, Mr. Smith)* Because *Mr. Smith* is already restricted, the participial phrase is not necessary to restrict it, so commas are necessary.

Write on the board: The man driving to school had an accident.

Ask students, do you know which man had an accident? (*No*) The participle is necessary to restrict *man* and commas should not be used.

This concept is also studied in Level 2 with adjective clauses.

Infinitives

Before reading the explanation in the workbook, write the following sentences on the board. In these sentences, the infinitive is the verbal with the sign of the infinitive *to*. Ask students to tell you about the infinitives (used like a noun, adjective, or adverb). Infinitive means *not limited.* Ask students how these sentences prove that.

1. Laurie likes to play the piano. (*direct object*)
2. To take money is stealing. (*subject*)
3. Sam's ambition is to fly. (*subject complement*)
4. His job, to wash cars, exhausts him. (*apposition*)
5. Joe was about to leave home. (*object of preposition*)
6. They had no water to drink. (*modifies adjective*)
7. He was anxious to go home. (*modifies adverb*)

The study of infinitives used like nouns is another review of case. These exercises can be gone over quickly, but it is important that students recognize the infinitive and use it correctly.

Omission of the Sign of the Infinitive

The noun or pronoun that precedes an infinitive is always in the *objective* case.

Her mother made *her clean* her room.

Her mother made her to clean her room.

The entire phrase *her clean* is the object of *made,* not just *her.* The basic pattern would be *mother made her clean room.*

Students have learned that the subject controls the verb, not the noun in front of an infinitive.

The verbal that precedes an infinitive is in the objective case.

Go over the explanation in the workbook. Work **Exercise 146** orally with the students to reinforce what you have just explained.

Correct usage is important. Drill by using both subject complement and infinitive complement.

Write the following on the board and ask students to explain the difference.

The most popular boy is he.

The teachers thought the most popular boy is he.

The teachers thought the most popular boy to be him.

Drill this concept until students understand it.

"I Like to See It Lap the Miles" by Emily Dickinson uses infinitives effectively. Put the poem on a transparency and go over the infinitives with the students. The entire poem is one sentence with all the infinitives used as direct objects of *like.*

Test

Level 1—Unit 7
Verbals

Test
Level 1—Unit 7
Verbals

Name ____________________

Date ____________________

Directions: Write *G* for gerund, *P* for participle, or *I* for infinitive. Then write the use of the gerund, the word the participle modifies, or the part of speech of the infinitive.

___ 1. Emily likes hearing her name.

___ 2. Ann saw the tiny tot coasting down the hill.

___ 3. Having sung the song, we left the stage.

___ 4. They observed her teaching a first grade class.

___ 5. She wants him to write the letter.

___ 6. I remember hearing the dreadful sound.

___ 7. I recommend this type of reading.

___ 8. I dare you to send that letter.

___ 9. Jean likes to draw on colored paper.

___ 10. Creating destruction and havoc, the wind brought fear to everyone.

___ 11. Joe's quitting his job was known by his fellow workers.

___ 12. Faced with the facts, the man confessed to the murder.

___ 13. You saw it grow gradually dark.

___ 14. His job, working at the post office, gives him good money.

___ 15. My boss was studying to go to law school.

___ 16. Her car stolen, she notified the police.

___ 17. The principal knew nothing of her winning the prize.

___ 18. Kicking off his shoes, Tom slumped in his chair.

___ 19. Disgusted, his mother glowered at the mess.

___ 20. The boy standing at the bus stop is Phillip.

___ 21. Sailing is my favorite sport.

___ 22. Their dog showed signs of training.

___ 23. This is no time to start.

___ 24. Wrapping the gifts took a long time.

___ 25. Mary enjoys gardening.

___ 26. John likes to sing in the choir.

___ 27. My father enjoys the art of painting.

___ 28. Having finished our chores, we left.

___ 29. The girl skating on thin ice is my sister.

___ 30. Shopping is often tiring.

___ 31. I enjoy shopping.

___ 32. John likes to shop.

___ 33. My favorite sport is walking.

___ 34. Joe's profession, advertising, is very competitive.

___ 35. The teacher wants me to write an essay.

___ 36. Jean works hard to earn a scholarship.

___ 37. To believe often takes great faith.

___ 38. The box wrapped with a red ribbon is for you.

___ 39. The chemist, choked by the fumes, fainted.

___ 40. The teacher ordered me to leave.

Level 1 Final Examination

Name ______________________

Date ______________________

Part A.

Directions: For each verb, write *INT* for intransitive, *TR* for transitive, or *L* for linking.

___ 1. The boys in the room played chess during the noon hour.

___ 2. The students were very competitive.

___ 3. Everyone in the class enjoyed the game.

___ 4. My favorite sport is baseball.

___ 5. We practice every day from 3:00 to 6:00 P.M.

___ 6. Our coach is very strict.

___ 7. The team worries before each game.

___ 8. After winning, we usually celebrate at the pizza place.

___ 9. Baseball requires skill and perseverance.

___ 10. It is enjoyed by all types of people.

___ 11. My sister likes playing volleyball.

___ 12. Volleyball is also a boys' sport.

___ 13. Most high schools sponsor a boys' volleyball team.

___ 14. Soccer, basketball, and tennis are played by both girls and boys.

___ 15. All of these sports require athletic ability and physical stamina.

Part B.

Directions: Write *N* for nominative case or *O* for objective case for the italicized nouns and pronouns.

___ 16. Tom is a great *leader* in his class.

___ 17. After the *show*, we plan to attend the concert.

___ 18. To my friends, *Tom* and *Pete*, the rewards were given.

___ 19. It could have been *he* in the room.

___ 20. The *wind* was blowing fiercely last night.

___ 21. Jim, the best tennis *player* in the league, won a trip to Hawaii.

___ 22. They sent *Jack* the book.

___ 23. To the *winner* much praise was given.

___ 24. We all decided to leave early in the *morning*.

___ 25. The process of finding the problem was a painful *one*.

Part C.

Directions: Write the letter of the correct answer.

___ 26. Everyone thought the best student to be (A. he B. him).

___ 27. How did that medicine (A. affect B. effect) your appetite?

___ 28. She is (A. sure B. surely) a good teacher.

___ 29. This desk feels very (A. smooth B. smoothly).

___ 30. The number of accidents last week (A. was B. were) five.

___ 31. Of the two winners in the essay contest, Ed is the (A. best B. better).

___ 32. Not one of the examples on either test (A. was B. were) easy to understand.

___ 33. A number of desks (A. was B. were) shipped to another school.

___ 34. How many of you heard of (A. they B. their) moving to Indiana?

___ 35. She (A. lay B. lays) the dishes on the table every day.

___ 36. The best singer would be (A. she B. her).

___ 37. Let's you and (A. I B. me) report the accident to the police.

___ 38. Everyone wants (A. he B. him) to join the Naval Academy.

___ 39. Ted was (A. lying B. laying) by the fire during the storm.

___ 40. Please (A. bring B. take) this material to the librarian.

___ 41. Mary looks like (A. she B. her) in that picture.

___ 42. Neither Jane nor Mervin (A. have B. has) been in this office all day.

___ 43. Every one of her classmates except Edna and (A. I B. me) was invited to the picnic.

___ 44. (A. We B. Us) freshmen will help decorate the gym for the class party.

___ 45. Each of the women had (A. her B. their) own success story to relate.

Answers to Workbook Exercises Level 1

Unit 1

Exercise 1

1. Pete and Jim skated all weekend.	*Pete, Jim skated*
2. A box of tomatoes lay on the porch.	*box lay*
3. Jerry walked to the Oaks Mall.	*Jerry walked*
4. Come in from the rain.	*(you) come*
5. Walk carefully over that debris.	*(you) walk*
6. The papers fell to the floor.	*papers fell*
7. Our team practiced last Saturday night.	*team practiced*
8. Bob ate quickly and went to class.	*Bob ate, went*
9. The coach and the team celebrated in Hawaii.	*coach, team celebrated*
10. The girls enrolled in a painting class.	*girls enrolled*
11. The class went on a picnic.	*class went*
12. Please walk carefully on the wet floor.	*(you) walk*
13. The class laughed at the joke.	*class laughed*
14. Her mother left in anger.	*mother left*
15. Beatrice cried to herself.	*Beatrice cried*
16. The teacher smiled at his antics.	*teacher smiled*
17. Peter and John went on a fishing trip.	*Peter, John went*
18. The dog ran around the room.	*dog ran*
19. Jane writes well.	*Jane writes*
20. Brian sang on the stage.	*Brian sang*
21. My friend left last night for Japan.	*friend left*
22. Lori worked hard all day.	*Lori worked*
23. My brother sat quietly in his chair.	*brother sat*
24. Pete ran into the house.	*Pete ran*
25. Jim spoke clearly and forcefully.	*Jim spoke*

Exercise 2

1. They camped beside the creek.	*they camped*
2. Jerry left in the morning.	*Jerry left*
3. Paul sang for his friends.	*Paul sang*
4. Pete and Jim rested.	*Pete, Jim rested*

Sentence	Answer
5. John stood across the street.	*John stood*
6. Our team walked five miles yesterday.	*team walked*
7. She ate in the rain.	*she ate*
8. Leave quietly.	*(you) leave*
9. Drive carefully near the school grounds.	*(you) drive*
10. The leaves fell to the ground.	*leaves fell*
11. Maria went to Mexico.	*Maria went*
12. Bob works at the Oaks Pharmacy.	*Bob works*
13. Go to your room.	*(you) go*
14. Peter yelled at his brother.	*Peter yelled*

Exercise 3

Sentence	Answer
1. My fountain pen writes better every day.	*pen writes*
2. The old Indian squatted solemnly.	*Indian squatted*
3. The leaf drifted slowly to the ground.	*leaf drifted*
4. Mary waited patiently for the bus.	*Mary waited*
5. The door closed quietly behind him.	*door closed*
6. Robert painted in the dark.	*Robert painted*
7. Jane swam in Jack's swimming pool.	*Jane swam*
8. She works for money.	*she works*
9. My cat crawled down the hall.	*cat crawled*
10. Bill ran away from home.	*Bill ran*
11. Bernice walked into the library.	*Bernice walked*
12. Please dust behind your desk.	*(you) dust*
13. The team practiced hard all afternoon.	*team practiced*
14. My mother went with me to the dentist.	*mother went*
15. Walk carefully on the wet floor.	*(you) walk*
16. Lily spoke slowly.	*Lily spoke*
17. Bob rode around the field.	*Bob rode*
18. Jill sang during intermission.	*Jill sang*
19. Tim swims every day.	*Tim swims*
20. Mary squealed in fright.	*Mary squealed*

Exercise 4

Sentence	Answer
1. Jane dug among the lilies.	*Jane dug*
2. The old man fumbled with the house key.	*man fumbled*
3. The boy walked down the road with his dog.	*boy walked*
4. On Saturday afternoon, the circus came to our town.	*circus came*
5. Four noisy little boys played joyfully in the park.	*boys played*
6. In his comfortable chair sat my grandfather.	*grandfather sat*
7. In a hurry, Jane ran across the busy street.	*Jane ran*
8. Our team will play next week.	*team will play*
9. My mother worked in the hot kitchen all day.	*mother worked*

10. The driver fled from the accident.	*driver fled*
11. My teacher left in a hurry.	*teacher left*
12. Mount Vesuvius erupted in a cloud of fire.	*Mount Vesuvius erupted*
13. Kelly studied for the test.	*Kelly studied*
14. Our kite rose quickly into the sky.	*kite rose*
15. The crew worked feverishly in the hot sun.	*crew worked*
16. Our new table arrived yesterday.	*table arrived*
17. The boys were standing on the porch.	*boys were standing*
18. A ten-speed bike rolled down the hill.	*bike rolled*
19. A flock of crows settled in our yard.	*flock settled*
20. Jack studied in his room.	*Jack studied*

Exercise 5

Note: The complete modifier may include articles and adjectives.

1. dug among lilies
2. fumbled with key
3. walked down road with dog
4. came to our town
   on Saturday afternoon
5. played joyfully in park
6. sat in chair
7. ran in hurry across street
8. will play next week
9. worked in kitchen all day
10. fled from accident
11. left in hurry
12. erupted in cloud
13. studied for test
14. rose quickly into sky
15. worked feverishly in sun
16. arrived yesterday
17. were standing on porch
18. rolled down hill
19. settled in yard
20. studied in room

Exercise 6

Original sentences

Exercise 7

1. I	6. N	11. N	16. I
2. I	7. I	12. I	17. I
3. I	8. I	13. I	18. N
4. I	9. I	14. I	19. N
5. I	10. N	15. N	20. I

Exercise 8

1. My sister bought a new dress yesterday.	*sister bought dress*
2. Finish your homework.	*(you) finish homework*
3. Our team won the championship.	*team won championship*
4. She wrote a letter to my father.	*she wrote letter*
5. She broke her arm during practice.	*she broke arm*
6. The team must practice football after school.	*team must practice football*
7. Our English class held a debate.	*class held debate*
8. Mary finished her essay.	*Mary finished essay*

9. Take this book to the library.	*(you) take book*
10. Jerry and Bob will wax the floors tomorrow.	*Jerry, Bob will wax floors*
11. Karen read the novel in one evening.	*Karen read novel*
12. Jane typed her composition carefully.	*Jane typed composition*
13. Byron found his book on the table.	*Byron found book*
14. Tom wore his best suit to the concert.	*Tom wore suit*
15. Arthur sold his best painting.	*Arthur sold painting*
16. Debra lost an earring during the dance.	*Debra lost earring*
17. Bill bought a pizza for lunch.	*Bill bought pizza*
18. John wrote a short story for his English class.	*John wrote story*
19. Ted had an accident last night.	*Ted had accident*
20. Julie wrote her essay on a computer.	*Julie wrote essay*

Exercise 9

1. The dog bared his teeth and growled.	*dog bared teeth, growled*
2. Greg ordered two hamburgers and fries.	*Greg ordered hamburgers, fries*
3. Stewart wrote an excellent essay.	*Stewart wrote essay*
4. Our old car needs a thorough overhauling.	*car needs overhauling*
5. My friend will visit me next week.	*friend will visit me*
6. At halftime our band played several numbers.	*band played numbers*
7. Tom hurt his arm during football practice.	*Tom hurt arm*
8. My friends and I enjoyed the movie very much.	*friends, I enjoyed movie*
9. Wash the windows and woodwork in your room.	*(you) wash windows, woodwork*
10. The baseball hit him on the head and broke his glasses.	*baseball hit him, broke glasses*
11. My brother borrowed Dad's car and went to a dance.	*brother borrowed car, went*
12. June read five novels last month.	*June read novels*
13. Kelly left her books at the beach.	*Kelly left books*
14. My cousin won a prize for her essay.	*cousin won prize*
15. Before lunch, Sarah washed her blouse.	*Sarah washed blouse*
16. My favorite horse won the race on Saturday.	*horse won race*
17. The boys painted the fence for Mr. Jones.	*boys painted fence*
18. My mother and her friends visited the children in the hospital.	*mother, friends visited children*
19. Finish the assignment quickly.	*(you) finish assignment*
20. Call your mother to the phone.	*(you) call mother*

Exercise 10

Part A.

1. Early Saturday morning, we put the food for the families into the truck.
2. The students had brought many different kinds of canned food.
3. The truck had plenty of room for everything.
4. Club members had also gathered several boxes of clothing.
5. The boys grabbed the boxes and put them into the truck.
6. The principal gave us money for turkeys.
7. We also bought vegetables and fruit.
8. At the last minute, the janitor came with Christmas trees.
9. We had already collected ornaments for the trees.
10. The families will have a wonderful Christmas.

Part B.

Original sentences

Exercise 11

Part A.

I removed my dirty tennis shoes and stepped cautiously into the creek. The cold water tickled my toes and sent shivers up my spine. I saw tiny minnows nearby. I raised my hand and brushed a low overhanging branch out of my way. A few twigs caught my hair. Suddenly, I stepped on a rock and fell. I pulled myself to a sitting position and looked around. I had sprained my ankle. It was throbbing painfully. I crawled to the end of the creek and pulled myself out of the water. I sat on the bank and cried. My father found me about two hours later, carried me home, and tucked me into bed. His hugs and kind words comforted me, and I soon fell asleep.

Part B.

Original paragraphs

Exercise 12

1. INT where
2. TR letter
3. TR accident
4. INT when
5. TR pigeons
6. INT how
7. TR way
8. TR knot
9. TR friend
10. INT where
11. INT when
12. TR pencil
13. TR cake
14. TR floor
15. TR marbles
16. INT where
17. TR duet
18. INT where
19. TR arm
20. TR way
21. INT where
22. TR contest
23. TR Jerry
24. INT how
25. TR books
26. INT where
27. INT when
28. TR error
29. TR thief
30. TR mistake
31. INT when
32. TR nothing
33. TR ball
34. INT when
35. TR dress
36. TR sweater
37. TR breakfast
38. INT how
39. TR elbow
40. TR leg
41. INT how
42. INT where
43. INT how
44. TR garden
45. INT when
46. TR nail
47. TR test
48. INT when
49. TR course
50. INT when

Exercise 13

Original sentences

Exercise 14

1. A message was sent to his brother.
2. The windows were washed.
3. My algebra book was stolen.
4. The dishes were put on the table.
5. The solo is sung beautifully.
6. The door was opened.
7. The boy was caught.
8. My car keys were taken.
9. The package was delivered.
10. My brother was grabbed.

Exercise 15

1. A reward was earned by Agnes.
2. Baseball was played.
3. The kitchen will be cleaned by Ruth.
4. The trail was lost by the hikers.
5. The song was sung by Tom.
6. The reason was found by the doctors.
7. Mabel's cookbook was published.
8. Gas for the car was bought by Jim.
9. The grass was mowed by my little sister.
10. Sue's geometry book was sold.
11. The rug was vacuumed by her brother.
12. A home run was hit by John.
13. Chocolate is loved by Joey.
14. The wall was papered by Jack and his cousins.
15. Nothing was found.
16. Two loaves of bread were baked by Suzanne.
17. My homework was destroyed by our dog.
18. The typewriter was broken by John.
19. A party was planned by the senior class.
20. My video camera was stolen.

Exercise 16

1. D	6. R	11. D	16. D
2. R	7. D	12. D	17. R
3. R	8. D	13. R	18. D
4. D	9. R	14. D	19. R
5. R	10. D	15. R	20. R

Exercise 17

1. The order was sent to his friend in Kentucky.
2. Father sent the money by express.
3. The librarian sold the old books.
4. Three new computers were bought by the principal.
5. Father painted our house last summer.
6. The maintenance workers will repair the classroom later in the year.
7. A new umbrella should be bought.
8. Our swimming pool was damaged by floods.
9. Someone stole my new video.
10. The exam paper was signed by my teacher.
11. The living room drapes will be washed by my mother.
12. Father's car was damaged by Bob.
13. A hit-and-run driver hit the girl.
14. Your letter will by typed by her.
15. Jane will buy the drinks.
16. This report should be written by you by Friday.
17. I returned the overdue library books.
18. The package was sent express by him.
19. Last month she cleaned drapes.
20. An earthquake destroyed our house.

Exercise 18

1.	TR	A	8.	INT	A	15.	INT	A	22.	TR	A
2.	INT	A	9.	TR	P	16.	TR	P	23.	TR	P
3.	TR	P	10.	TR	A	17.	TR	A	24.	TR	P
4.	TR	A	11.	TR	A	18.	TR	A	25.	TR	A
5.	TR	A	12.	TR	A	19.	INT	A			
6.	INT	A	13.	INT	A	20.	INT	A			
7.	INT	A	14.	INT	A	21.	TR	A			

Exercise 19

Book in hand, I headed [INT] for my favorite reading place. I walked [INT] quickly along in the cold water. I eyed [TR] the shells, crabs, seaweed, jellyfish, and other seaside treasures. Finally, I arrived [INT] at my destination, a large black jetty jutting far out into the sea. I climbed [TR] the smooth boulder and walked [INT] out to the end. I did not observe [TR] the rising tide, the white caps, and the black clouds creeping inland. I sat [INT]on my favorite rock at the end of the jetty, reading. I did not hear [TR] the waves lapping higher on the rocks.

Suddenly I saw [TR] a flash of lightning and heard [TR] an earth-shaking clap of thunder. I put TR my book over my head and began [TR] the long run off the jetty. Panic gripped [TR] my muscles. The tide had come [INT] in and poured [INT] over the middle of the jetty. I was confronted [TR] with the ocean just a few yards away. Instinctively, I climbed [TR] the rock, but the water lapped [INT] further up the rock and swirled [INT] madly around my ankles. I cried [INT] out in fear. Then I heard [TR] an engine and saw [TR] a Coast Guard helicopter. By means of a rope I was hoisted [TR] into the helicopter. I looked [INT] down and saw [TR] a wave roll over my rock, taking with it my book. I turned [INT] away as a cloud hid [TR] the sight from my view.

Exercise 20

Original sentences

Exercise 21

1. Jane washed the dishes.
2. After the game, hamburgers were brought for everyone by us.
3. During intermission, several numbers were played by our band.
4. The pen was broken by Alice.
5. Miss Jones read my composition.
6. During a volleyball game, Jean's arm was broken.
7. Ruth's blouse was washed and ironed.
8. We found money under the floor.
9. The Rolling Stones are loved by Eleanor.
10. Nothing was done about the accident by the officers.
11. The first-place tennis trophy was won by John.
12. The cake was baked and frosted by Nancy.
13. The election was lost by Jill.
14. Tennis was played by Jean all mornng.
15. He returned my books before class.
16. The storm broke my window.
17. My sister collected miniature elephants.
18. A tap dance was danced by Collette in the variety show.
19. Crying accomplished nothing.
20. We saw that video three times.

Exercise 22

1. Loggers stripped the trees last month.
2. The company shipped the computers in September.
3. My brother wrote the letter.
4. My brother drove the old car.
5. The janitor repaired the school bell in September.
6. A robber stabbed the man.
7. Mother took my shoes to the shoemaker.
8. The storm uprooted the trees.
9. He stained the bookcase a dark walnut.
10. In March we planted flowers.

Exercise 23

1. The classroom door was fixed by the janitor.
2. My photograph was taken by Mr. Smith.
3. The algebra test was passed by all the students.
4. Twenty percent of the games were lost by our basketball team.
5. Our kitchen was renovated by the contractor.

6. The school song was composed by Jane Beard.
7. Two keys on her typewriter were broken.
8. Pictures were taken at the picnic by my father.
9. The animals are loved by the zookeeper.
10. Tom's license was taken by the judge.

Exercise 24

Note: The paragraph can be rewritten with the following changes in verb form.

Darkness shrouded the corridor. Huge doors of dark wood lined the hall. The cold morning air seeped through the cracks and chilled my bones. The floor creaked with each step, adding to my fears. *A strange sense of disaster confronted me. Darkness veiled everything.* Gathering my courage, I timidly knocked on the enormous door. It opened slowly. *A kind-looking person welcomed me.* He took my hand and brought me into a beautiful parlor. "You are a new boarder here at Anaheim Military Academy. You are welcome," he said. *"You will have a student guide to show you around the school.* He will take care of you." My high school career had just begun.

Exercise 25

1.	Who <u>wrote</u> in my book?	INT
2.	Our football team <u>practiced</u> all morning.	INT
3.	The campers <u>feared</u> the bears.	TR
4.	My sister <u>waited</u> at the depot for three hours.	INT
5.	The spectators <u>cheered</u> for their team.	INT
6.	Kevin <u>pitched</u> horseshoes with his uncle.	TR
7.	The little kitten <u>followed</u> us.	TR
8.	John <u>enjoys</u> mystery stories.	TR
9.	The author <u>typed</u> all morning.	INT
10.	The rain <u>fell</u> steadily all day.	INT

Exercise 26

1. L	7. L	13. TR	19. L
2. TR	8. TR	14. TR	20. TR
3. L	9. L	15. TR	21. L
4. TR	10. TR	16. TR	22. TR
5. TR	11. TR	17. L	
6. L	12. L	18. L	

Exercise 27

Original sentences

Exercise 28

1. L	6. L	11. TR	16. TR
2. L	7. TR	12. TR	17. L
3. TR	8. TR	13. L	18. TR
4. L	9. L	14. L	19. TR
5. L	10. TR	15. L	20. L

Exercise 29

Original sentences

Exercise 30

1. L
2. L
3. TR
4. TR
5. TR
6. L
7. L
8. L
9. TR
10. L
11. L
12. TR
13. L
14. L
15. L
16. TR
17. L
18. TR
19. L
20. L

Exercise 31

1. PT
2. L Harry might be president next year.
3. PT
4. PT
5. L Ted was my friend.
6. PT
7. L The top of my desk was very rough.
8. L Betty seemed very ill.
9. PT
10. PT
11. L Jane looks very worried.
12. L Bill's uncle is a doctor.
13. L My sister will be tired.
14. PT
15. PT
16. L John was very happy about the award.
17. L John will be a mechanical engineer someday.
18. PT
19. L Jerry has been an honor student all year.
20. PT

Exercise 32

Original sentences

Exercise 33

1. TR (A)
2. L
3. TR (P)
4. INT
5. L
6. TR (A)
7. TR (P)
8. INT
9. L
10. L
11. INT
12. TR (P)
13. TR (A)
14. L
15. L
16. INT
17. TR (A)
18. L
19. TR (P)
20. L

Exercise 34

Pizza is [L] the perfect food. I could eat [TR] it every day. All four food groups are represented. [INT] I like [TR] vegetables on mine, but some people prefer [TR] cheese and pepperoni. Pizza places are [L] everywhere, and best of all, they deliver. [INT]

Exercise 35

Original sentences

Exercise 36

1. TR	6. INT	11. TR	16. TR
2. TR	7. TR	12. TR	17. TR
3. L	8. TR	13. INT	18. L
4. TR	9. TR	14. TR	19. L
5. TR	10. L	15. L	20. L

Unit 2

Exercise 37

1. future	8. future	15. present
2. past perfect	9. past perfect	16. past
3. present perfect	10. present perfect	17. past perfect
4. past	11. future	18. present
5. present	12. present	19. past perfect
6. present	13. future	20. past
7. future perfect	14. future perfect	

Exercise 38

1. Jerry walks to school each morning. *present*
2. I will vacuum the rug later. *future*
3. My mother has worked there for two years. *present perfect*
4. We decided to go to the basketball game. *past*
5. The class chose James as their mascot. *past*
6. My parents have already left for New York. *present perfect*
7. Dave eats lunch in the cafeteria at noon. *present*
8. My brother plays in the park every Saturday. *present*
9. Bob will give you my address later. *future*
10. She had shopped yesterday. *past perfect*

Exercise 39

1. was (were) finding	5. is (are) choosing
2. will be giving	6. is (are) singing
3. was choosing	7. had been speaking
4. has been writing	8. is speaking

9. was speaking
10. will be leading
11. was writing
12. was seeing
13. has been sending
14. had been rising
15. was blowing
16. was enjoying
17. has been seeing
18. will have been tearing
19. was tearing
20. is going
21. is jogging
22. had been studying
23. has been tearing
24. will have been tearing
25. is burning
26. has been enjoying

Exercise 40

1. Jill is working for my father.	*works*
2. The birds were flying overhead.	*flew*
3. Sarah will be giving her report tomorrow.	*will give*
4. Sean has been playing football for the past three years.	*has played*
5. Cindy is writing the music for the show.	*writes*
6. My brother was enjoying the play.	*enjoyed*
7. The boys were riding their bicycles.	*rode*
8. She has been singing in the choir all year.	*has sung*
9. John will be entering college in the fall.	*will enter*
10. Tom is studying chemistry.	*studies*
11. My cousin will be playing the saxophone.	*will play*
12. My friend and I have been skiing.	*have skiied*
13. James will be sending his final report card to his mother.	*will send*
14. We were eating lunch early.	*ate*
15. Jesse has been contacting his lawyer.	*has contacted*
16. I will be learning to sew.	*will learn*
17. We were planning a trip to Africa.	*planned*
18. Mother will soon be preparing dinner.	*will prepare*
19. His father was painting the house.	*painted*
20. They were going to the game.	*went*

Exercise 41

Original verbs

Exercise 42

Original sentences

Exercise 43

1. The note for my absence was (signed) by my mother.
2. The gates of the U.S. Embassy were (closed) at 8:00 P.M.
3. The water will be (turned) off in the morning.
4. Her bedroom had been (painted) last week.
5. Jane's typewriter was (purchased) by her father.

6. The uses of that product <u>have</u> <u>been</u> (studied) thoroughly.
7. All the materials <u>were</u> (removed) from the table.
8. Her books <u>had</u> <u>been</u> (taken) to the library.
9. The principal's report <u>will</u> <u>be</u> (given) tomorrow.
10. The news <u>was</u> (given) out very cautiously.
11. The taxi <u>had</u> <u>been</u> (called).
12. The little old man <u>was</u> (injured) in a fall.
13. The microphones <u>were</u> (set up) in the auditorium.
14. The various articles <u>will</u> <u>be</u> (sorted) by the social committee.
15. Mr. Johnson's lawn <u>was</u> (mowed) by Tim.
16. The papers <u>were</u> (corrected) by the teacher.
17. Her office <u>was</u> (painted) last year.
18. The computer <u>has</u> <u>been</u> (repaired).
19. A computer <u>was</u> (bought) for our English class.
20. Her bracelet <u>was</u> (stolen) last night.

Exercise 44

1. P	8. PRO	15. L	22. L
2. L	9. L	16. PRO	23. P
3. P	10. L	17. L	24. PRO
4. P	11. P	18. P	25. L
5. PRO	12. PRO	19. PRO	
6. PRO	13. L	20. P	
7. P	14. P	21. P	

Exercise 45

1. The teacher took my paper and *wrote* several comments.
2. She found the book on the sidewalk and *returned* it to the teacher.
3. Mary saw the accident and *called* the police.
4. The museum is open seven days a week but the library *is* not.
5. The policeman keeps a close watch on all activities and immediately *reports* anything unusual.
6. Terry ran into the house and *saw* her mother on the floor.
7. I turned the key and *started* the car.
8. Mr. Jones painted my room and *left* his brushes on my desk.
9. Tom took his book to the library and *sat* down to read the newspaper.
10. Mother cleaned my room and *threw* away my term paper.

Exercise 46

Check that verbs are either in the present or past tense.

Exercise 47

1. Tom *loses* his way in the forest.
2. She *has sung* on the stage many times.
3. He *had seen* that show before.
4. Joan *laughed* at the joke.
5. She *will buy* several articles at the Price Club.
6. Joan *took* the flowers to her friend in the hospital.
7. Robert *has given* his time most generously.
8. The boys *went* on a long trip last week.
9. The wind *had blown* fiercely all night.
10. My little brother *ate* the entire pie.
11. Tim *rides* his bike to school each morning.
12. Shirley *has lost* her book.
13. She almost *broke* the vase.
14. Lori *had stolen* the material from her friends.
15. John *will write* the letter tomorrow.
16. She *left* the room.
17. We *visited* our Uncle Bill yesterday.
18. Joe *has worked* for his uncle.
19. She *rises* from her chair.
20. Jane *had chosen* the material for her prom dress.

Exercise 48

Original sentences should include the following verbs

1. take(s) *or* is taking
2. will go *or* shall go
3. had written
4. has (have) finished
5. has (have) taught
6. had taken
7. was rising
8. will be writing
9. does sing
10. is flying
11. did go
12. had sent
13. will bring
14. has (have) broken
15. was writing
16. has (have) taken
17. will paint
18. has (have) walked
19. drew
20. was drawing

Exercise 49

Original sentences should include the following verbs

1. is (are) given
   or is (are) being given
2. will be written
3. have (has) been bought
4. had been shipped
5. will be broken
6. was left
7. is (are) chosen
   or is (are) being chosen
8. was stolen
9. had been rung
10. has (have) been seen
11. is cut *or* is being cut
12. will be built

Exercise 50

1. How long will Tom *lie* in bed this morning?
2. He has *lain* there too long.
3. Albert was *lying* in the sun all morning.
4. The teacher *laid* her books on her desk.
5. Now her books are *lying* on her desk.
6. The lecturer was *laying* his papers on the podium.
7. Now his papers are *lying* on the podium.
8. Pete *lay* on the grass and cried.
9. My dog is *lying* on the rug.
10. The doctor *lays* his forceps on the table.
11. They *lay* there all morning.
12. Robert *laid* the cover over his pool.
13. Now the cover was *lying* over his pool.
14. He was *laying* the cover over his pool.
15. Tom had *laid* the shells in the sun.
16. He was *lying* in the sun.
17. He *lies* there for an hour.
18. Jim *laid* his pencils near his typewriter.
19. Now his pencils are *lying* near his typewriter.
20. Mildred is *lying* on her bed.
21. She was *lying* there for over an hour.
22. I *lay* the book down.
23. I also *laid* it down yesterday.
24. I had *laid* it there very often.
25. She had been *laying* scraps of paper all over the floor.

Exercise 51

1. sat
2. let
3. set
4. sitting
5. sat
6. raised
7. sit
8. risen
9. leave, let
10. leave
11. let
12. rose
13. let
14. raised
15. leave
16. set
17. let
18. Let
19. setting
20. lets
21. Set
22. let
23. leaves
24. rose
25. sat

Review Test on Verbs

Part A.

1. We found the car keys yesterday. *transitive, active, past*
2. Andrew will leave tomorrow. *intransitive, active, future*
3. Has Tom finished his work? *transitive, active, present perfect*
4. His suit will be pressed later. *transitive, passive, future*
5. Jane took his remarks seriously. *transitive, active, past*
6. This building is earthquake-proof. *linking, present*

7. We all heard the loud noise.	*transitive, active, past*
8. Pete will work on his new project.	*intransitive, active, future*
9. The team will win the next game.	*transitive, active, future*
10. Charles' book of poems was published.	*transitive, passive, past*
11. The baby is quiet now.	*linking, present*
12. We have had that bill for two weeks.	*transitive, active, present perfect*
13. They will participate in the debate.	*intransitive, active, future*
14. She is an expert driver.	*linking, present*
15. Kathy is a remarkable young lady.	*linking, present*
16. The books had been delivered.	*transitive, passive, past perfect*
17. The boy will soon learn his lesson.	*transitive, active, future*
18. Jane shuts the window quietly.	*transitive, active, present*
19. Ralph was standing next to me.	*intransitive, active, past progressive*
20. Fred and I will finish the job soon.	*transitive, active, future*
21. Mary will never find the package.	*transitive, active, future*
22. Bob burned all his bridges.	*transitive, active, past*
23. The report was destroyed.	*transitive, passive, past*
24. Albert will probably fail algebra.	*transitive, active, progressive*
25. The airplane was flying overhead.	*intransitive, active, past progressive*

Part B.

1. laying	6. lying	11. leave	16. raised
2. Let	7. sat	12. lying	17. sat
3. sat	8. let	13. laid	18. set
4. lying	9. let	14. lay	19. Let
5. lays	10. raised	15. let	20. lying

Part C.

1. The computer was fixed.
2. They repainted the lockers during the summer.
3. The gym floor was refinished by the janitor.
4. She took all her belongings to the office.
5. They had cleaned the carpets in the classrooms.
6. The reports were filed according to dates by Albert.
7. The musical Sunset Boulevard was enjoyed by everyone.
8. New equipment was added to our science lab this year.
9. The SAT will be taken by Jerry in November.
10. New books for our library will be ordered by the librarian.
11. They transplanted the flowers.
12. A new sweater has been sent to each of us by Aunt Julie.
13. They will order the flowers later.
14. They finally repainted the house.

Part D.

Students should keep the tense of the verbs consistent.

Unit 3

Exercise 52

1. pianos	6. churches	11. halves (of)	16. boxes
2. echoes	7. bushes	12. rules-of-thumb	17. alumni
3. data	8. mothers-in-law	13. potatoes	18. giraffes
4. stars	9. chairmen	14. teeth	19. fathers-in-law
5. branches	10. knives	15. crises	20. mice

Exercise 53

1. Brian with his three sisters visited Europe last summer. *Brian visited Europe*
2. In my room was a shelf of mystery stories. *shelf was*
3. The photographer with his wife has left for Hawaii. *photographer has left*
4. A sack of oranges was delivered to the cafeteria. *sack was delivered*
5. A bottle of syrup broke on my clean kitchen floor. *bottle broke*
6. The principal gave us a longer lunch period. *principal gave period*
7. The coach, with his assistants, wants a victory. *coach wants victory*
8. In the second race, our team finally won. *team won*
9. Nothing satisfied him. *nothing satisfied him*
10. The photographer took pictures of the students. *photographer took pictures*

Exercise 54

1. Mrs. Traverse, the (secretary) at our school, retired last fall.
2. Paul Jones, the yearbook (editor) of Seraph Scrolls, will graduate in June.
3. Jane Coffman, the (winner) of the music contest, received a trip to Boston.
4. Tom and Pete, my best (friends), went to England.
5. My scissors, an (heirloom), cut the ribbon for the grand opening of the museum.
6. My mother, a flower (lover), spends many hours in her garden.
7. Pete, the (janitor), painted the gym in one week.
8. Apricots, my favorite (fruit), also make a good pie.
9. John, the (captain) of our football team, received a scholarship to Penn State.
10. Bob, the (master) of ceremonies, has a tremendous sense of humor.

Exercise 55

1. C	6. C	11. A	16. S
2. S	7. C	12. A	17. A
3. A	8. C	13. C	18. S
4. A	9. A	14. A	19. C
5. S	10. S	15. C	20. S

Exercise 56

1. Jack left the room very angry
2. Bob saw his friend at the theater.
3. We bought paper and pencils for the exam.
4. Everyone applauded the man's efforts to rescue his brother.
5. The class wrote a letter to the President of the United States.
6. Marie saw her little sister in the park.
7. The newsboy found his papers in the bushes.
8. The minister led his congregation in song.
9. Ted sold his bike to the first customer.
10. Peg led the bikers on a new trail.
11. Our class had a Christmas party.
12. Joan strung Christmas lights in her porch.
13. Someone stole Jack's bicycle.
14. We all welcomed the new teacher.
15. File these papers today.
16. Listen to the flute.
17. The guide took us on a hike in the woods.
18. Where did you find that wallet?
19. We noticed the boy's reluctance to speak.
20. Send me the teacher's report.

Exercise 57

1. The principal gave the (class) a free period.
2. Ships brought the (people) food and clothing.
3. The Thespian Club gave the (school) a great movie.
4. The baker made my (mother) several loaves of bread.
5. The FBI sent (Mr. Matthews) a warning.
6. The photographer gave the (school) several free photographs.
7. Please take (Mary) and (Ted) some ice cream.
8. The Constitution guarantees (Americans) their freedom.
9. The freshman class gave the basketball (team) hot chocolate.
10. My friend offered (Mrs. Smith) his car.
11. We certainly gave (Miss Jones) a fright.
12. Mr. Benson gave his (nephew) nothing for his birthday.
13. Mrs. Newhall wrote her (son) a letter every day.
14. Please give (Joan) this note.
15. I gave my (father) my good report card.
16. Mr. Johnson sent his (son) some money.
17. The policeman gave (me) a ticket for speeding.
18. A walk each day will give the (invalid) some exercise.
19. Albert sent his (mother) flowers for Mother's Day.
20. My Aunt Nellie sent (me) my favorite recipe.

Exercise 58

1. IO
2. A
3. A
4. A
5. IO
6. IO
7. A
8. IO
9. DO
10. DO
11. DO
12. IO
13. IO
14. IO
15. DO
16. IO
17. A
18. DO
19. DO
20. DO

Exercise 59

1. The girl in the blue (dress) is my sister.
2. The freshmen on our football (squad) look unusually big and tall.
3. The old house was made of (adobe).
4. The students in her (class) must speak French.
5. During the (war) my brother was injured by a (grenade).
6. The men from the construction (company) attended the rally.
7. The airplane flew above the (clouds).
8. We walked around the (block) and across the train (tracks).
9. A chattering squirrel scampered up the (tree).
10. Clare's initials are engraved inside her (ring).
11. The ship sailed at (midnight).
12. A light rain fell during the (night).
13. Mildred remained in her (room) all day.
14. The garage stands between the (house) and the (barn).
15. We divided the fruit among the four (boys).
16. The crew lowered the lifeboats into the (water).
17. The lecture covered a variety of (subjects).
18. All may leave but (Tom).
19. After the (battle) the soldiers rested for one (week).
20. Many trees were destroyed during the (storm).
21. He has found leaders among (men) of (thought) and (action).
22. They came in the summer (months) by (hundreds).
23. The team emerged from the (game) victorious and unscathed.
24. Our judgments concerning his (worth) were biased.
25. Their wives seldom go to the (island) before (May).

Exercise 60

1. A
2. A
3. A
4. B
5. B
6. B
7. B
8. B
9. B
10. A
11. A
12. B
13. B
14. B
15. A
16. B
17. A
18. A
19. A
20. B
21. B
22. B
23. B
24. A
25. B

Exercise 61

Original sentences

Exercise 62

Original phrases

Exercise 63

Last summer we took a trip to Hawaii. We packed plenty of swimsuits and suntan lotion. It takes a long time to get there, so we also brought plenty of magazines to read during the flight. When we arrived in Honolulu, we rented a car and drove to our hotel. That night we took a long walk on the beach, which was only a block from our hotel. The next morning, we went swimming in the ocean. After lunch at the hotel restaurant, we visited two museums. Then we drove around the city and saw some sights before dinner.

Later that week, we took a submarine ride in a coral reef. The boat went through schools of brightly colored tropical fish, and we watched two scuba divers feed them. Another interesting place we visited was the Pearl Harbor memorial, which is built over a sunken ship in the harbor. You can even see parts of the ship underneath you.

After two weeks of fun in the sun, it was time to go home. We bought plenty of souvenirs and took lots of pictures so we will always remember our vacation and the good time we had.

Exercise 64

Original sentences

Exercise 65

1. Please take this *box with the red bow* to Miss Campos.
2. *Maps of the city* were given to the tourists.
3. My little brother fed the dog *food in the green box* to his dog.
4. That *book on the table* belongs to Jerry.
5. *At our weekly assembly,* Mr. O'Neill told us all about his adventures in Africa.
6. *At the assembly, we* promised the principal to speak quietly in the halls.
7. The *box with the red bow* was wrapped by Pete.
8. *At the rally,* we supported our basketball team with many cheers.
9. Our *piano with the wooden legs* was sold by my brother.
10. My *car with dirty windows* was inspected by my friends.

Exercise 66

1. boys'
2. girl's
3. men's
4. geese's
5. John's
6. babies'
7. boss's
8. book's
9. leaders'
10. day's
11. calf's
12. coach's
13. authors'
14. child's
15. bride's
16. week's
17. pencil's
18. Tom's
19. month's
20. mice's
21. dress's
22. books'
23. table's
24. woman's
25. baby's
26. sister's
27. lady's
28. pitcher's
29. deer's
30. army's

Exercise 67

1. men's	6. mouse's	11. bread's	16. hour's
2. Joan's	7. children's	12. umpire's	17. sister's
3. stone's	8. woman's	13. turkeys'	18. book's
4. mother's	9. sweater's	14. salesmen's	19. enemies'
5. Tom's	10. cousin's	15. Peter's	20. month's

Exercise 68

1. my parents' farm
2. Jim's skates
3. one hour's delay
4. the librarian's request
5. the men's club
6. the girl's bicycle
7. the bird's nest
8. the coach's orders
9. Dickens's novels
10. the teachers' reply
11. the ladies' dresses
12. Jerry's ball
13. Janice's bracelet
14. the baby's crib
15. the judge's verdict
16. the editor's pamphlets
17. Ibsen's plays
18. Shakespeare's comedies
19. Eliot's poems
20. the parents' problems

Exercise 69

1. Brian and Rob's
2. Arthur's, Jeff's
3. Wilson's, Roosevelt's
4. Jason's, Jean's
5. Kilmer's, Rossetti's
6. Tom and Bob's
7. Jean's, Nell's
8. husband and wife's
9. judge's, lawyer's
10. Mrs. Jones and Mrs. Zoll's
11. Mary and her brother's
12. Kevin and Brian's
13. Jean and her sister's
14. Paul's, John's
15. Cindy's, Tom's
16. Jack's, Terry's
17. Jimmy's, parents'
18. Bessie's, uncle's
19. Tess and Jack's
20. principal's, teachers'

Exercise 70

1. Friday is *Lincoln's* birthday.
2. We are taking geometry and *Science* III this year.
3. The *Union Trust Bank* installed a new security system.
4. We drove south to see one of the *South's* most important crops.
5. Our history course this year is *History* 4A.
6. Judge *Smith* exonerated Jack Brennan with no hesitation.
7. We spoke with *President* Bush.
8. We traveled two miles north and three miles west to visit the site of the *Olympics*.
9. My *father's* store is two miles away.
10. Mr. Morgan was all smiles and good wishes on the birthday of *ex-Senator* Smith.

11. In spring my mother and father will visit the *ex-governor* of California.
12. Two women in the group, Miss Jones and Miss Brown, knew two of *Keats's* poems.
13. We mailed the order to the *American Bank.*
14. We plan to visit *Aunt* Mary and *Uncle* Tom today.
15. We bought a copy of the *New Testament.*
16. Have you ever seen the *Grand Canyon*?
17. My *mother's* favorite aunt will visit next week.
18. We visited my uncle on the *Fourth* of *July.*
19. We will study the *Civil War* as juniors.
20. Shelley belonged to the *Romantic Movement.*

Exercise 71

1. The 1900s brought tremendous inventions, exciting events, and new ideas to the United States. *Correct*
2. In December 1903, *Orville* and Wilbur *Wright* startled the world with their first flying experience.
3. In 1904, over 20,000 visitors came to the *St. Louis World's Fair* to marvel at the hundreds of exhibits that proved that America was on the move.
4. Athletes from all over the world competed in the *Olympic Games* held in conjunction with the *St. Louis World's Fair.*
5. The *American Baseball League* was formed in 1901, introducing a new level of competition for this very popular sport.
6. On *Independence Day,* July 4, there were parades, concerts, picnics, and fireworks.
7. In 1906, the first mass-produced *Fords* were marketed.
8. *The Jungle,* a book by Sinclair Lewis, helped to bring about the *Pure Food and Drug Act* in 1906.
9. Many "quack" medical cures came to a quick halt. *Correct*
10. With the turn of the century, *America* entered a new age, now called the *Progressive Era.*

Exercise 72

Carlos *Gomez,* president of the *Spanish Club* at *Jefferson High School,* organized a program for *Cinco* de *Mayo.* Because many students in the school were of *Mexican* or *Native American* background, this day was very popular with the students. After a special luncheon of *carne* asada tortillas, and *guacamole,* the students assembled in the auditorium for a program of dances by different groups of *Hispanic* girls and boys. At the end of the program, Mr. *Cordena, principal* of the school, showed us a video that he had taken while on a trip to *Mexico* during the past summer.

Exercise 73

Note: Style books may vary on the capitalization of titles of high office used alone as in number 4.

1. She moved to *Beacon Street* last week.
2. A committee of the *House* of *Representatives* wrote the agenda.

3. My *father* is a member of the *Democratic Party.*
4. I wrote to the postmaster general about his lack of cooperation. *Correct*
5. The sophomore class is quite spirited this year. *Correct*
6. John wasn't from the *South* as he claimed.
7. I learned that he was staying at the *Hilton Hotel* in Hawaii.
8. Hilda, a junior from *Germany,* is a top-ranking tennis player.
9. Have you ever lived in *Temple City*?
10. Unlike ice skating, roller skating is not a winter sport. *Correct*
11. Robert lives in the southwest part of the *country.*
12. What did you do on *Labor Day*?
13. If you want to attend Palo Alto *High School,* you need a recommendation.
14. Doctor Hansen spoke at the *Rotary Club* meeting.
15. Doctor Hubert Manning, a Baptist *minister,* led the invocation.
16. Our senior class decided to visit the *Smithsonian Institution* during our Easter vacation.
17. Our *American* history class spoke with *ex-Governor* Johnson.
18. *Governor-elect* Martin is an astute politician.
19. To be *secretary* of state you must be a tough politician.
20. We saw Mr. Whitehead, the *principal* of Wellington *High School,* at a special meeting of principals from this area.
21. The teachers visited *John Hamilton High School* last fall.
22. During the summer we went to see the *Lincoln Memorial* in Washington, D.C.
23. She plans to study *chemistry* and *physics* as a *junior* and *senior* in high school.
24. My *mother* wants to visit the *South* next year to see the tobacco farms.
25. She has lived in *Thousand Oaks* for the past ten years.
26. We have to travel west in order to visit *Aunt* Jane.
27. Judge Alvarado was appointed secretary of state during the month of March. *Correct*
28. The *president* of the *gas company* sent me a memo in *August.*
29. Have you ever read the books of the *Bible*?
30. We studied *Buddhism,* as well as *Hinduism,* in college.

Exercise 74

1. B	8. A	15. A	22. B
2. A	9. B	16. A	23. B
3. B	10. A	17. A	24. A
4. B	11. A	18. B	25. A
5. A	12. A	19. B	
6. B	13. A	20. A	
7. B	14. A	21. A	

Exercise 75

1. B	4. B	7. A	10. B
2. B	5. B	8. A	
3. A	6. A	9. A	

Exercise 76

1. There were several reasons for his actions.
2. Here is your new assignment.
3. There is a notice of dismissal in your mailbox.
4. There's nothing in the box.
5. Here's your apple.
6. There's no reason for such conduct.
7. Here are your mother's instructions.
8. There's no point to this argument.
9. Here's my excuse.
10. There's his blue sweater.

Exercise 77

1. His one desire is acting and singing in a musical comedy.	*desire is acting and singing*
2. My mother's favorite fruit is apples.	*fruit is apples*
3. The reason for his dislike of school is his many demerits.	*reason is demerits*
4. Tom's choice of a good luncheon is cheese sandwiches.	*choice is sandwiches*
5. The movie's appeal is its realistic characters.	*appeal is characters*

Exercise 78

1. B	4. A	7. B	10. A
2. A	5. B	8. A	
3. B	6. A	9. B	

Exercise 79

1. A	4. B	7. B	10. B
2. A	5. A	8. A	
3. B	6. A	9. A	

Exercise 80

1. B	10. A	19. B	28. B
2. A	11. A	20. A	29. B
3. B	12. A	21. A	30. B
4. B	13. B	22. A	31. A
5. A	14. B	23. A	32. A
6. A	15. B	24. B	33. A
7. A	16. A	25. A	34. B
8. B	17. A	26. B	35. A
9. B	18. A	27. A	

Unit 4

Exercise 81

1. I	4. it	7. you	10. we
2. we	5. he	8. I	
3. she	6. they	9. he	

Exercise 82

1. I	4. he	7. we	10. they
2. they	5. she	8. you	
3. I	6. he	9. she	

Exercise 83

1. A	6. A	11. A
2. A	7. A	12. B
3. B	8. B	13. A
4. A	9. B	14. A
5. A	10. A	15. A

Exercise 84

1. B	6. A	11. A
2. B	7. A	12. A
3. B	8. A	13. B
4. B	9. B	14. B
5. B	10. A	15. A

Exercise 85

1. us	O	4. she	N	7. we	N	10. him	O
2. her	O	5. we	N	8. they	N		
3. he	N	6. me	O	9. she	N		

Exercise 86

1. OI	8. OI	15. OI	22. OD
2. OD	9. OD	16. NC	23. NS
3. NS	10. OI	17. OD	24. OI
4. OD	11. OI	18. OI	25. OI
5. NS	12. NC	19. OI	26. NS
6. OI	13. OD	20. OI	27. OI
7. NS	14. OI	21. NC	28. OD

Exercise 87

1. B	6. A	11. A	16. B
2. B	7. B	12. B	17. B
3. B	8. A	13. A	18. A
4. A	9. A	14. B	19. B
5. B	10. B	15. A	20. A

Exercise 88

Original sentences

Exercise 89

1. mine	8. mine	15. hers	22. its
2. yours	9. our	16. their	23. ours
3. mine	10. your	17. yours	24. mine
4. hers	11. their	18. his	25. their
5. theirs	12. its	19. his	
6. our	13. its	20. his	
7. my	14. mine	21. my	

Exercise 90

Original sentences

Exercise 91

Pronouns will vary, but should be in the following cases.

1. Objective	6. Nominative
2. Possessive	7. Objective
3. Nominative	8. Objective
4. Objective	9. Possessive
5. Possessive	10. Objective

Exercise 92

Pronouns will vary, but should be in the following cases.

1. Objective	6. Objective
2. Nominative	7. Objective
3. Objective	8. Possessive
4. Nominative	9. Possessive
5. Objective	10. Possessive

Exercise 93

1. <u>Mary</u> did it to herself.	*R*
2. <u>Mary</u> herself will go to the mall.	*I*
3. <u>Marshall</u> <u>Foch</u> planned the strategy himself.	*I*
4. My little <u>sister</u> can dress herself.	*R*
5. <u>I</u> myself will plan the dance.	*I*

6. She can do it herself. *I*
7. My father cut himself with his razor. *R*
8. She bruised herself during the basketball game. *R*
9. My mother does everything herself. *I*
10. The players enjoyed themselves at the barbecue. *R*
11. We ourselves will do the work. *I*
12. She sent the reports to the insurance company herself. *I*
13. She looked at herself in the mirror. *R*
14. Jean gave the eulogy herself. *I*
15. Did the prisoner enjoy himself yesterday? *R*
16. I could not lift the package by myself. *R*
17. The teacher herself praised us for our work. *I*
18. I myself have never questioned his loyalty. *I*
19. My father himself will attend the next meeting. *I*
20. I poured myself a cup of coffee. *R*
21. My little brother went to the park by himself. *R*
22. We enjoyed ourselves at the football game. *R*
23. The principal himself gave us a free day. *I*
24. She herself asked for the job. *I*
25. John loves himself. *R*

Exercise 94

1. is
2. was
3. has
4. is
5. his
6. was
7. was
8. is
9. is
10. is

Exercise 95

1. are
2. are
3. are
4. were
5. are
6. need
7. were
8. are
9. are
10. are

Exercise 96

1. has
2. were
3. is
4. were
5. were
6. have
7. were
8. was
9. were
10. were

Exercise 97

1. has
2. is
3. is
4. have
5. plan
6. wants
7. are
8. is
9. has
10. plans

Exercise 98

1. who
2. who
3. whom
4. whom
5. whom
6. whom
7. who
8. whom
9. whom
10. who
11. whom
12. who
13. whom
14. whom
15. whom

Exercise 99

1. A	10. A	19. A	28. A
2. B	11. B	20. A	29. B
3. A	12. B	21. A	30. A
4. A	13. B	22. B	31. A
5. A	14. B	23. B	32. A
6. A	15. B	24. B	33. A
7. B	16. B	25. B	34. A
8. A	17. A	26. A	35. A
9. B	18. A	27. B	

Exercise 100

1. A	14. A	27. B	40. A
2. A	15. A	28. A	41. A
3. A	16. A	29. B	42. A
4. A	17. A	30. A	43. B
5. A	18. B	31. B	44. B
6. A	19. B	32. A	45. A
7. B	20. A	33. B	46. B
8. B	21. B	34. A	47. A
9. A	22. A	35. B	48. A
10. A	23. B	36. B	49. A
11. B	24. B	37. A	50. A
12. A	25. B	38. B	
13. A	26. B	39. B	

Exercise 101

Sentence	Answer
1. Everybody in the room send you his love.	*sends*
2. Neither my book report nor my essay are finished.	*is*
3. Either my father or my mother wants to leave early.	*Correct*
4. Neither the coach nor the players hopes to win the game on Saturday.	*hope*
5. Neither Bob or his sister plans to go skiing on Saturday.	*nor*
6. Gymnastics has always appealed to me.	*Correct*
7. Many a man and woman have problems with relationships.	*has*
8. The number of errors on this paper are too high.	*is*
9. Either Jill or her sister is planning a reunion.	*Correct*
10. The number of places in the auditorium are not enough.	*is*
11. Measles for older people are very serious.	*is*
12. The extra practice helped us win.	*Correct*
13. A number of reunions is planned for this summer.	*are*
14. Two-thirds of the cake have been eaten.	*has*
15. Sixty-five cents is missing.	*Correct*
16. Either my boss or his managers is ruining the business.	*are*

17. Each of the dogs are well-groomed for the show. *is*
18. Trumps is important in the game. *are*
19. Most of the players has part-time jobs. *have*
20. Molasses makes everything sticky. *Correct*
21. Another cause of the accident were the unpaved roads. *was*
22. The number of voters in the last elections were very small. *was*
23. The data was not sufficient for her research paper. *were*
24. Riches often brings unhappiness. *bring*
25. A shelf of books in her bedroom have broken under the weight. *has*
26. His study of economics was rewarding. *Correct*
27. Three-fifths of the problem were solved. *was*
28. A number of accidents occurs on Pacific Coast Highway. *occur*
29. *The Grapes of Wrath* are a great novel. *is*
30. A bunch of grapes were given to each child. *was*
31. Each of the papers on the desk were ruined by water. *was*
32. My father's pliers were stolen from his garage. *Correct*
33. The principal with a few of his faculty are planning to meet on Friday. *is*
34. Seventy-five cents is too much to pay. *Correct*
35. The news in the paper concerning the flood were very discouraging. *was*
36. His trousers needs pressing. *need*
37. His ashes was distributed over the ocean. *were*
38. Can you and I leave early tomorrow morning? *Correct*
39. Five dollars were the cost of the scissors. *was*

Unit 5

Exercise 102

1. A mystery book was stolen from our library.
2. His book was found in the trash bin.
3. Two British airplanes flew over our heads.
4. Whose watch was lost last night during the basketball game?
5. Many students attended the Youth Convention in Anaheim last month.
6. Our class saw a fascinating movie in our American history class.
7. We saw four large turtles, each weighing over one hundred pounds.
8. My brother visited several museums on his long tour of Europe.
9. The second girl from the left received a special prize.
10. David entered the third race at the class picnic.

Exercise 103

1. Kodak, Alaska
2. Correct
3. Greek
4. anti-Panama

5. East, Buddhist
6. Spanish-speaking Americans, California
7. Norman, Britain
8. Chinese
9. Russian
10. Renaissance
11. John F. Kennedy Memorial Library
12. Theater of Fine Arts
13. Chief Justice, Supreme Court (style books may vary for *chief justice*)
14. Huntington Museum
15. ex-Senator Smith

Exercise 104

1. C	6. M	11. M	16. C
2. C	7. C	12. M	17. C
3. M	8. M	13. C	18. M
4. C	9. M	14. M	19. M
5. C	10. C	15. M	20. C

Exercise 105

1. S	6. S	11. C
2. S	7. S	12. C
3. C	8. S	13. S
4. C	9. S	14. C
5. S	10. S	15. S

Exercise 106

1. better, best
2. more wonderful, most wonderful
3. more handsome, most handsome
4. larger, largest
5. bigger, biggest
6. kinder, kindest
7. sadder, saddest
8. warmer, warmest
9. stricter, strictest
10. happier, happiest
11. smoother, smoothest
12. more brilliant, most brilliant
13. healthier, healthiest
14. braver, bravest
15. more successful, most successful

Exercise 107

1. B	6. B	11. A	16. B
2. B	7. A	12. B	17. B
3. B	8. B	13. B	18. B
4. B	9. B	14. B	
5. B	10. B	15. A	

Exercise 108

1. The coat I bought last week is warmer than *Jane's.*
2. The Beatles were greater than any *other* group of musicians.
3. Driving in the winter requires more caution than *driving in the summer* (or *in the summer*)
4. John was more focused than any *other* player on the team.
5. Jill works harder than anyone *else* in the class.
6. Cornflakes is more nutritious than any *other* brand.
7. Jack is more ambitious than anyone *else* in his family.
8. Barb reads more mystery stories than anyone *else.*
9. The milk of a goat is richer than a *cow's.*
10. Today's weather is warmer than *yesterday's.*
11. The sophomores' ideas for the dance are much better than the *seniors'.* (or *those of the seniors*)
12. These directions for assembling a radio are less complicated than *those for assembling* a tricycle.

Unit 6

Exercise 109

1. The Indians moved silently through the forest.	how
2. We all looked up.	where
3. Slowly she walked into her room.	how
4. Sing again, Rosemarie.	when
5. Have you ever visited Valley Forge?	when
6. My brother now lives in Boston.	when
7. The parrot chattered noisily.	how
8. Speak distinctly.	how
9. You have answered the question wisely.	how
10. She plays the organ well.	how
11. Robert, please step down.	where
12. You may come in.	where
13. Edward whistled cheerfully.	how
14. The carpenter had already completed his work.	when
15. Her spirit will never die.	when
16. My father drives cautiously.	how
17. My parents have gone away for the weekend.	where
18. William carefully checked his answers.	how
19. The bus stops here.	where
20. He ran quickly into his house.	how
21. The train sped onward.	where
22. The boy fell down.	where
23. The speedboats swiftly skimmed over the water.	how
24. The frightened boy jumped back.	where
25. The old man walked awkwardly across the room.	how

Exercise 110

1. extremely, happy	6. exceedingly, pale
2. barely, visible	7. very, tragic
3. visibly, upset	8. generally, kind
4. unusually, loud	9. somewhat, unhappy
5. partially, correct	10. positively, wrong

Exercise 111

1. Margaret slept very <u>soundly</u> in her new bed.	*very*
2. Rita plays the violin extremely <u>well</u>.	*extremely*
3. She works too <u>slowly</u> for my taste.	*too*
4. The speaker spoke most <u>eloquently</u>.	*most*
5. I cleaned my room somewhat <u>carefully</u>.	*somewhat*
6. My little brother reads very <u>well</u>.	*very*
7. Rita just <u>barely</u> finished her breakfast on time.	*just*
8. The jury reached its verdict unexpectedly <u>early</u>.	*unexpectedly*
9. The bus ran surprisingly <u>fast</u>.	*surprisingly*
10. The cookies were almost <u>completely</u> gone.	*almost*

Exercise 112

1. ADV	6. ADJ	11. ADV	16. ADJ
2. ADJ	7. ADJ	12. ADJ	17. ADJ
3. ADJ	8. ADV	13. ADV	18. ADV
4. ADV	9. ADJ	14. ADJ	19. ADV
5. ADJ	10. ADV	15. ADV	20. ADJ

Exercise 113

Answers may vary.

Exercise 114

1. A	5. A	9. A	13. B
2. B	6. B	10. B	14. A
3. B	7. B	11. B	15. B
4. B	8. A	12. B	

Exercise 115

1. A	6. B	11. B	16. B
2. A	7. A	12. B	17. A
3. B	8. A	13. A	18. B
4. B	9. B	14. A	19. B
5. A	10. B	15. A	20. A

Exercise 116

1. John doesn't know nothing about my problem.	*John doesn't know anything about my problem.*
2. I can't do nothing.	*I can't do anything.*
3. I don't have none.	*I don't have any.*
4. She couldn't hardly take a step.	*She could hardly take a step.*
5. She couldn't scarcely swim.	*She could scarecely swim.*
6. There is hardly no time to finish my essay.	*There is hardly any time to finish my essay.*
7. There was scarcely no food in the house.	*There was scarcely any food in the house.*
8. I don't want nothing.	*I don't want anything.*
9. We couldn't find no receipt.	*We couldn't find any receipt.*
10. His mother wouldn't let him have none.	*His mother wouldn't let him have any.*

Exercise 117

1. Mary ran very quickly down the street.
2. Slowly she lifted the glass to her lips.
3. Awkwardly, he pulled the blanket over his little sister.
4. The corn grew quite rapidly in the hot sun.
5. Back and forth the angry man walked.
6. Tom spoke rapidly and angrily.
7. The deer ran directly toward the man.
8. He pushed the dish forward on the table.
9. He could hardly see the screen.
10. It is not time yet.

Exercise 118

1. A
2. E
3. A
4. E
5. A
6. E
7. A
8. A
9. A
10. E

Exercise 119

1. adverb, marched
2. adjective, children
3. adverb, did
4. adverb, left
5. adjective, prairie
6. adverb, did
7. adjective, picnic
8. adverb, disappeared
9. adjective, improvement
10. adverb, work
11. adjective, seat
12. adverb, went
13. adjective, girl
14. adjective, quiz
15. adverb, arrived
16. adjective, country
17. adjective, poster
18. adverb, leaves
19. adjective, bird
20. adverb, come
21. adjective, worker
22. adverb, earned
23. adjective, worker
24. adjective, she
25. adjective, table

Exercise 120

1. Mary plays the piano good. — *well*
2. My brother felt some better after the workout. — *somewhat*
3. The cake smells so deliciously. — *delicious*
4. She is the better player on the team. — *best*
5. I really felt badly at the loss of the game. — *bad*
6. Study the two chapters close. — *closely*
7. Janette is sure correct most of the time. — *surely*
8. I didn't know nothing about the problem. — *anything*
9. My friend was some disturbed over his error. — *somewhat*
10. The school bell sounds noisily all day. — *noisy*
11. Brian felt good enough to go to the concert. — *well*
12. My father was some disturbed over my grades. — *somewhat*
13. Her dress is no different than mine. — *from*
14. Bob is the better tennis player in the class. — *best*
15. She certainly writes good. — *well*
16. He walked very quick to school. — *quickly*
17. I have no need for his assistance. — *of*
18. I can't do nothing about the situation. — *anything*
19. Neither Jane or Jessie has finished the assignment. — *nor*
20. Mary is the brighter of the three girls. — *brightest*

Exercise 121

Answers may vary.

Unit 7

Exercise 122

1. Working on that bridge was a dangerous undertaking. — *working was undertaking*
2. Dropping your pencil during class can be very distracting. — *dropping pencil can be distracting*
3. Throwing water balloons during lunch hour is forbidden. — *throwing balloons is forbidden*
4. Working for my boss, Mr. Jones, is a real challenge. — *working is challenge*
5. Lying in bed on Sunday morning is very relaxing. — *lying is relaxing*
6. Singing in our glee club requires much practice. — *singing requires practice*
7. Praising others is a good habit. — *praising others is habit*
8. Sitting in that chair is very uncomfortable. — *sitting is uncomfortable*
9. Washing clothes is an easy chore. — *washing clothes is chore*
10. Playing the piano is her favorite hobby. — *playing piano is hobby*

Exercise 123

1. Each of the girls must finish cleaning her room by Friday.	*each must finish cleaning room*
2. She dislikes studying math.	*she dislikes studying math*
3. We enjoyed listening to your sermon.	*we enjoyed listening*
4. Captain Jones enjoys cooking in his spare time.	*Captain Jones enjoys cooking*
5. He likes telling stories about his fishing experiences.	*he likes telling stories*
6. Tony considered flying for a career.	*Tony considered flying*
7. Our English professor enjoys telling jokes.	*professor enjoys telling jokes*
8. Jean hates speaking in public.	*Jean hates speaking*
9. My little sister likes hiking and skiing.	*sister likes hiking, skiing*
10. Mrs. Peters considered crocheting a quilt for the auction.	*Mrs. Peters considered crocheting quilt*

Exercise 124

1. His ability, playing several instruments, is enjoyed by many.
   ability (playing instruments) is enjoyed
2. Her job, working in the May Company, is sometimes boring.
   job (working) is boring
3. My one desire, becoming an actress, seems very remote.
   desire (becoming actress) seems remote
4. The fact, knowing the extent of the damage, should be his first priority.
   fact (knowing extent) should be priority
5. His specialty, playing the guitar, brought him some lucrative opportunities.
   specialty (playing guitar) brought opportunities
6. His job, selling insurance, brings him much satisfaction.
   job (selling insurance) brings satisfaction
7. Her one hope, going to England, will soon be realized.
   hope (going) will be realized
8. Molly's favorite activity, hiking up mountains, can be dangerous.
   activity (hiking) can be dangerous
9. My sister's new appointment, working at Gray's Photography, has many opportunities.
   appointment (working) has opportunities
10. My summer job, working as a receptionist, is not easy.
    job (working) is easy

Exercise 125

1. of standing
2. after finishing the assignment
3. by choosing the captain
4. by working
5. of studying
6. without removing boots
7. by rescuing the dog
8. between going
9. for riding the waves
10. by reading

Exercise 126

1. The man's chief responsibility was going to work. *responsibility was going*
2. My brother's work was running errands all day. *work was running errands*
3. Her hobby is knitting. *hobby is knitting*
4. Her job each evening is washing the dishes. *job is washing dishes*
5. Her mother's job was teaching first graders. *job was teaching graders*
6. His favorite sport is swimming. *sport is swimming*
7. Alfred's greatest honor was winning the race. *honor was winning race*
8. My greatest fear is running out of gas on the freeway. *fear is running*
9. Molly's favorite pastime is reading. *pastime is reading*
10. One of Mary's hobbies is collecting penguins. *one is collecting penguins*

Exercise 127

1. G	5. P	9. P	13. P
2. P	6. G	10. G	14. G
3. P	7. P	11. P	15. G
4. P.	8. G	12. G	

Exercise 128

1. S	8. DO	15. SC	22. S
2. SC	9. A	16. S	23. SC
3. DO	10. OP	17. S	24. OP
4. DO	11. OP	18. DO	25. A
5. OP	12. S	19. SC	
6. OP	13. S	20. DO	
7. OP	14. DO	21. SC	

Exercise 129

Original sentences

Exercise 130

A gerund is a *verbal noun.* It has *one* form. Gerunds add *-ing* to the *present* tense of the verb. A gerund can be used as a *subject, direct object, subject complement, apposition,* or *object of preposition.* Use the *possessive* case to modify a gerund if the noun is *posessive.*

Three examples of this are
1. *my receiving*
2. *his studying*
3. *Tom's earning.*

Exercise 131

1. Playing tennis, Tom sprained his ankle. *Tom*
2. That picture, seen by the entire class, was excellent. *picture*
3. Driving recklessly, Joe had an accident. *Joe*
4. Helping his mother clean the house, Joe earned a trip to the mountains. *Joe*
5. Paying attention to small details, Jean received a promotion. *Jean*
6. The bracelet purchased by my brother is truly a work of art. *bracelet*
7. Having washed the car, Bob joined his friends. *Bob*
8. Working on her computer, Mary produced an excellent essay. *Mary*
9. The material gathered for his term paper was not sufficient. *material*
10. Playing football in the park, Jerry hurt his leg. *Jerry*

Exercise 132

1. The old fence, whitewashed by the boys of the neighborhood, looks new. *fence*
2. The tires, worn thin by much driving, were replaced. *tires*
3. The telephone pole, snapped by the hurricane, almost hit our house. *pole*
4. Frightened by the cat, the bird flew away. *bird*
5. The essay written by my sister won first prize. *essay*
6. My car, stolen from the parking lot, was found last night. *car*
7. Sent by telegraph, the news was tragic. *news*
8. Found in the school yard, the wallet was returned to its owner. *wallet*
9. Surrounded by flowers, Jean laughed delightedly. *Jean*
10. Wounded by the car, my dog crawled into our yard. *dog*
11. Many voters, confused by the issues, did not vote. *voters*
12. Disgusted with the apathy of the players, the coach stormed out of the locker room. *coach*
13. The book, taken to the library by Bryan, was overdue. *book*
14. The full moon, seemingly suspended in the sky, was brilliant. *moon*
15. Exhausted by the strenuous game, the team relaxed. *team*
16. Chosen to represent the baseball team, Kevin went to San Francisco. *Kevin*
17. The blue vase, made by our art teacher, won several awards. *vase*
18. The package delivered by the mail carrier contained an important book. *package*
19. David, taken to the hospital, had a heart attack. *David*
20. The airplane flown by my cousin landed in Alaska. *airplane*

Exercise 133

1. P	8. P	15. G	22. P
2. G	9. G	16. G	23. P
3. G	10. G	17. G	24. G
4. G	11. P	18. P	25. G
5. P	12. G	19. P	
6. G	13. P	20. G	
7. P	14. P	21. G	

Exercise 134

1. P	6. P	11. P	16. P
2. P	7. P	12. V	17. P
3. V	8. V	13. V	18. V
4. P	9. V	14. P	19. V
5. P	10. P	15. P	20. P

Exercise 135

1. D	6. D	11. D	16. D
2. C	7. C	12. D	17. C
3. D	8. C	13. D	18. C
4. D	9. D	14. C	19. D
5. D	10. C	15. C	20. D

Exercise 136

Original sentences

Exercise 137

Original sentences

Exercise 138

1. N	6. R	11. N	16. N
2. N	7. R	12. N	17. N
3. N	8. N	13. R	18. R
4. R	9. R	14. N	19. R
5. R	10. N	15. R	20. N

Exercise 139

1. C	6. C	11. C	16. C
2. I	7. C	12. I	17. C
3. I	8. C	13. C	18. C
4. C	9. C	14. I	19. C
5. C	10. C	15. C	20. I

Exercise 140

	Sentence	Answer
1.	To write short stories was his one ambition.	*to write stories was ambition*
2.	To work hard is important for success.	*to work is important*
3.	To take good pictures is not always easy.	*to take pictures is easy*
4.	To have won success as a novelist is a great achievement.	*to have won success is achievement*
5.	To gain recognition in sports costs many hours of practice.	*to gain recognition costs hours*
6.	To speak about others is always unkind.	*to speak is unkind*
7.	To leave your room in disorder displeases your mother.	*to leave room displeases mother*
8.	To work for Tom is often difficult.	*to work is difficult*
9.	To have lost the way caused me a lot of worry.	*to have lost way caused worry*
10.	To sing in our choir is an exhilarating experience.	*to sing is experience*

Exercise 141

	Sentence	Answer
1.	Mary decided to take Jean, her sister, with her.	*Mary decided to take Jean (sister)*
2.	The coach needed to obtain permission from the principal.	*coach needed to obtain permission*
3.	Joan likes to study French.	*John likes to study French*
4.	They hope to move to Arizona.	*they hope to move*
5.	She decided to find the culprit herself.	*she (herself) decided to find culprit*
6.	He wants to leave for Mammoth immediately.	*he wants to leave*
7.	Bob would like to find his sister's bracelet.	*Bob would like to find bracelet*
8.	She hopes to send her son to college.	*she hopes to send son*
9.	John is determined to bring up his grades to a 3.0.	*John is determined to bring up grades*
10.	Margaret plans to go to college next year.	*Margaret plans to go*

Exercise 142

	Sentence	Answer
1.	The child did nothing except to gaze out of the window.	*except*
2.	Jane was about to sing a song.	*about*
3.	Brian desired nothing except to be left alone.	*except*
4.	I had no idea of how to locate him.	*of*
5.	Do you have any idea of where to find the article?	*of*
6.	The children were about to write their compositions.	*about*
7.	I had no idea of when to expect him.	*of*
8.	I was about to announce the winner.	*about*
9.	Bob was just about to leave the room.	*about*
10.	He did all the assignments except to write his final report.	*except*

Exercise 143

1. Albert's ambition is to become an artist. *ambition is to become artist*
2. Jenny's aim in life is to fly. *aim is to fly*
3. The art of reading is to scan judiciously. *art is to scan*
4. His hobby is to collect stamps. *hobby is to collect stamps*
5. Bill's intention was to leave home. *intention was to leave home*
6. Betty's one desire in life is to write a novel. *desire is to write novel*
7. The teacher's latest innovation will be to require five book reports a semester. *innovation will be to require reports*
8. My mother's job is to take care of ten small children. *job is to take care*
9. Tammie's purpose will be to motivate the children in their studies. *purpose will be to motivate children*
10. The manager's request was to do a day's work for a day's pay. *request was to do work*

Exercise 144

1. Our plan to publish the book did not succeed.
   plan (to publish the book) did succeed
2. Andy's command, to leave the room in order, was disobeyed.
   command (to leave room) was disobeyed
3. The general's report to send ten men immediately was issued yesterday.
   report (to send men) was issued
4. Joe's desire to go to the Olympics was finally realized.
   desire (to go) was realized
5. Her plan, to visit Hawaii this summer, met with her parents' approval.
   plan (to visit Hawaii) met approval
6. Bob's wish, to be admitted into the Naval Academy, should be realized.
   wish (to be admitted) should be realized
7. My sister's efforts to join the basketball squad succeeded.
   efforts (to join squad) succeeded
8. My father's job, to interview all applicants, was not always easy.
   job (to interview applicants) was easy
9. Melaina's efforts to do student teaching in inner-city schools succeeded.
   efforts (to do teaching) succeeded
10. The coach's intention to reach conference finals made him very strict.
    intention (to reach finals) made him strict

Exercise 145

1. Mr. Jones is the man to see. *man*
2. In this race, Mike is the one to beat. *one*
3. The campers had plenty of cold water to drink. *water*
4. Have you enough time to think? *time*
5. There were several good oranges to eat. *oranges*

6. There are two bottles of cold milk to drink. *milk*
7. Mr. Jones is the one to ask for an interview. *one*
8. This is an excellent pan to boil chicken. *pan*
9. Bob is the student to honor. *student*
10. She gave me a pear to eat. *pear*

Exercise 146

1. I	6. I	11. V	16. I
2. V	7. I	12. V	17. V
3. V	8. I	13. I	18. I
4. V	9. I	14. I	19. I
5. I	10. V	15. V	20. I

Exercise 147

1. her sing
2. to fly
3. to pass math
4. to relax
5. about to start
6. to observe
7. to watch game
8. to wash shirt
9. me know winner
10. dress to wear

Exercise 148

1. We thought the most glamorous person to be *her.*
2. They wanted *him* to leave immediately.
3. Everyone wanted *them* to perform at the concert.
4. We all *desparately* wanted *to help* the little girl.
5. To become a missionary *requires* require a sense of humor.
6. Professional skaters need *to practice daily.*
7. The teacher knew the culprit to be *him.*
8. Roxanne wanted *us* to see her in the play.
9. My friends wanted *her* to enter the contest.
10. My greatest desire is *to see* a good Shakespeare play.

Exercise 149

1. My wish is to help my brother go to college.
2. My friends urged me to join their sorority.
3. She always likes fresh apples to eat.
4. She wants to listen to country music.
5. I dared Joe (to) throw the snowball.
6. We all expected her to win the contest.
7. We all want Peter to run for class president.
8. Do you expect them to sponsor the senior class?
9. The principal believed the vandal to be him.
10. I wanted him to play in the school concert.

Answers to Unit Tests Level 1

Unit 1—Basic Patterns

1. INT	14. L	27. L	40. TR
2. TR	15. L	28. INT	41. TR
3. L	16. INT	29. TR	42. L
4. TR	17. TR	30. INT	43. TR
5. L	18. TR	31. INT	44. L
6. L	19. L	32. L	45. INT
7. INT	20. TR	33. TR	46. TR
8. TR	21. L	34. TR	47. TR
9. TR	22. TR	35. TR	48. L
10. TR	23. L	36. TR	49. TR
11. TR	24. INT	37. INT	50. TR
12. TR	25. L	38. L	
13. INT	26. INT	39. L	

Unit 2—Verbs

Part A.

1. past	6. past	11. past perfect	16. future
2. past perfect	7. present perfect	12. future	17. past perfect
3. future	8. past	13. present perfect	18. future
4. past	9. past	14. future perfect	19. present
5. past	10. present perfect	15. present progressive	20. present

Part B.

21. had found	23. gives, give, is giving	25. has lost	28. finished
22. will sing	24. chose	26. will take	29. took
		27. has accepted	30. tore

Part C.

31. wrote	34. had broken	37. brought	40. will see
32. plays	35. has torn	38. had eaten	
33. laughed	36. will lose	39. left	

Part D.

41. INT	44. L	47. TR	50. L
42. TR	45. TR	48. INT	
43. L	46. TR	49. TR	

Unit 3—Nouns

Part A.

1. OP	8. DO	13. OP	20. OP
2. N	9. IO	14. N	21. OP
3. OP	10. DO	15. N	22. OP
4. OP	11. OP	16. DO	23. OP
5. OP	12. SC (Note: open is an adjective)	17. OP	24. OP
6. SC		18. SC	25. SC
7. IO		19. OP	

Part B.

26. B	30. A	34. A	38. A
27. A	31. A	35. A	39. B
28. A	32. B	36. A	40. B
29. A	33. B	37. B	

Part C.

41. I	44. C	47. I	50. I
42. I	45. C	48. I	
43. C	46. C	49. C	

Unit 4—Pronouns

1. B	14. B	27. B	40. A
2. A	15. A	28. B	41. B
3. B	16. A	29. A	42. B
4. A	17. A	30. A	43. A
5. A	18. B	31. B	44. B
6. B	19. B	32. A	45. B
7. A	20. B	33. B	46. A
8. B	21. B	34. A	47. B
9. A	22. A	35. B	48. B
10. B	23. B	36. B	49. A
11. B	24. A	37. B	50. B
12. B	25. A	38. A	
13. B	26. A	39. A	

Unit 5—Adjectives

Part A.

1. S	4. C	7. S	10. C
2. C	5. S	8. P	
3. S	6. C	9. S	

Part B.

11. A
12. B
13. B
14. B
15. B
16. B
17. B
18. B
19. B
20. A

Part C.

21. C
22. C
23. M
24. M
25. C
26. M
27. M
28. C
29. M
30. C

Unit 6—Adverbs

Part A.

1. ADJ
2. ADV
3. ADJ
4. ADV
5. ADV
6. ADV
7. ADV
8. ADJ
9. ADV
10. ADV

Part B.

11. B
12. A
13. B
14. B
15. A
16. B
17. A
18. B
19. B
20. A
21. B
22. A
23. A
24. B
25. A

Unit 7—Verbals

1. G, direct object
2. P, tot
3. P, we
4. G, direct object
5. I, noun
6. G, direct object
7. G, object of preposition
8. I, noun
9. I, noun
10. P, wind
11. G, subject
12. P, man
13. I, noun
14. G, apposition
15. I, adverb
16. P, car
17. G, object of preposition
18. P, Tom
19. P, mother
20. P, boy
21. G, subject
22. G, object of preposition
23. I, adjective
24. G, subject
25. G, direct object
26. I, noun
27. G, object of preposition
28. P, we
29. P, girl
30. G, subject
31. G, direct object
32. I, noun
33. G, subject complement
34. G, apposition
35. I, noun
36. I, adverb
37. I, noun
38. P, box
39. P, chemist
40. I, noun

Level 1— Final Examination

Part A.

1. TR	5. INT	9. TR	13. TR
2. L	6. L	10. TR	14. TR
3. TR	7. INT	11. TR	15. TR
4. L	8. INT	12. L	

Part B.

16. N	21. N
17. O	22. O
18. O	23. O
19. N	24. O
20. N	25. N

Part C.

26. B	31. B	36. A	41. B
27. A	32. A	37. B	42. B
28. B	33. B	38. B	43. B
29. A	34. B	39. A	44. A
30. A	35. B	40. B	45. A

Level 2 Unit 1 Basic Materials

Objectives

- To review the basic concepts of Level 1
- To understand objective complement and nominative absolute

Pages 1–18; Exercises 1–15

Level 1 Review

Basic Patterns

Review the three basic patterns in the workbook. Drill by writing sentences on the board as you explain.

I ran down the road.

Jane sold her bicycle.

Bob is an expert golfer.

Have students write original sentences like the ones above. Suggest that they keep the sentences short.

Subject-Verb Agreement

Give **Exercise 3** as a quiz to determine weak points.

Case of Nouns and Pronouns

Have students put answers for **Exercises 4, 5,** and **6** on paper to determine any problems. Put students in small groups to correct their answers.

Verbals

Have students identify all of the verbals in **Exercise 7** before writing answers. Correct in groups. Divide the class in three groups with each group writing ten original sentences for one kind of verbal. Put the sentences on the board and have members of the group explain.

Phrases

Have students write original sentences for homework using all seven types of phrases.

Exercise 9 shows how phrases and modifiers add life to a sentence. After studying the explanation, do three or four on the board with the students. Have them do the rest for homework.

Objective Complement

This concept was not studied in Level 1, but it is not a difficult concept to teach. Before turning to the workbook, put the following sentence or one like it on the board:

My father painted my room a light green.

Ask students: What color was you room before your father painted it? What color is it now? Note for students that an adjective complement is not a modifier. Then write:

My room is a light green.

Ask students: What color is my room? In the first sentence, *light green* is a complement, telling what you painted the room; in the second sentence, *light green* is a modifier.

A complement always completes. In the following sentence, the complement completes a direct object; it is called an object complement.

We elected Tom captain.

Captain, the direct object, and *Tom*, the object complement, are the same person.

Put the following sentences on the board and explain them.

The teacher made Jane cocaptain. (noun)

We called the paper ours. (pronoun)

The accident made Jim a cripple. (adjective)

Work **Exercises 10–12**.

Nominative Absolute

It is important that students understand the meaning of *absolute*. Put this sentence or one like it on the board:

Mary ran into the room.

Ask the students to give you a participle modifying *Mary*, for example, "crying."

Mary *crying* ran into the room.

Ask students: What if I add, "her thumb cut and bleeding"? What is this phrase modifying? It is not connected grammatically to the sentence, so it is a nominative absolute. The noun is in the nominative case modified by a participle but connected only by meaning. Nominative absolutes do not modify any word in the basic pattern.

Test

Level 2—Unit 1
Basic Materials

Unit 1 should take about one quarter. If material is mastered earlier, start clauses.

Test

Level 2—Unit 1

Basic Materials

Name ______________________

Date ______________________

Part A.

Directions: Write *INT* for intransitive verbs, *TR* for transitive verbs, or *L* for linking verbs.

___ 1. My mother became ill over John's accident.

___ 2. The fumes made my brother dizzy.

___ 3. Tom did not see the speaker leave.

___ 4. The class worked diligently for over an hour.

___ 5. The computer class was basic.

___ 6. The materials were shipped last week to Japan.

___ 7. He tore his shirt playing football.

___ 8. Bill was a great tennis player.

___ 9. Tom liked to make everyone laugh.

___ 10. We saw nothing wrong in his actions.

___ 11. The class chose Willie for its mascot.

___ 12. Tillie has been a cheerleader for two years.

___ 13. The baseball team practiced for five hours on Saturday.

___ 14. Whom did she choose to represent her?

___ 15. They saw *Sense and Sensibility* three times.

Part B.

Directions: Underline the verbals in the following sentences. Write *G* for gerund, *P* for participle, *I* for infinitive, or *A* for absolute.

___ 16. Cheering loudly, the cheerleaders motivated the team.

___ 17. The old man literally dared me to break the window.

___ 18. To achieve success, you must be highly motivated.

___ 19. The balloon filled with water became a weapon.

___ 20. Ted wanted to leave immediately.

___ 21. The biggest joy of his life was flying with his uncle.

___ 22. Her hobby is knitting.

___ 23. Hair standing on edge, we crept into the dark damp cave.

___ 24. Gasping for breath, he was rushed to the emergency room.

___ 25. Studying physics, he earned his doctorate.

___ 26. His job was pitching for the New York Giants.

___ 27. He had a habit of noticing every beautiful scene.

___ 28. Head aching from the severe fall, Mike stumbled into the hospital.

___ 29. She asked to see our book.

___ 30. We want to watch this movie.

Part C.

Directions: Write the letter of the correct case.

___ 31. We all thought Tom to be (A. he B. him).

___ 32. Let's you and (A. I B. me) get going.

___ 33. Did you send (A. she B. her) the letter?

___ 34. The committee awarded (A. he B. him) the prize.

___ 35. Divide the papers between Joe and (A. he B. him).

___ 36. (A. Who B. Whom) did you see at the party?

___ 37. About (A. who B. whom) is she speaking?

___ 38. (A. We B. Us) boys are going to Hawaii during the summer.

___ 39. The teacher gave (A. we B. us) the good news.

___ 40. The best debater was surely (A. he B. him).

Part D.

Directions: For the italicized words, write *S* for subject complement, *O* for objective complement, or *D* for direct object.

___ 41. My little sister is already an excellent *golfer.*

___ 42. The committee named her an outstanding *golfer* last year.

___ 43. She received new golf *clubs* for an award.

___ 44. The news of his success made me *happy.*

___ 45. I lost all my *papers* during the storm.

___ 46. Her house was entirely too *small.*

___ 47. Joe called me an *extrovert.*

___ 48. My brother is the *extrovert* in our house.

___ 49. Did you meet my *mother* at the Anaheim Convention Center?

___ 50. The mayor appointed Janet *committee chairperson.*

Unit 2 Adverb Clauses

Objective

- To understand the adverb clause and subordination

Pages 19–34; Exercises 16–29

The first few pages of the unit explain the independent and the dependent clause. **Exercises 17** and **18** are a review of basics. After students understand the meanings of dependent and independent clauses, they are ready to study adverb clauses.

First, review adverbs by asking the students to tell you everything they remember about adverbs. Adverbs answer the questions *how, when, where, why, to what extent,* and *in what manner.* They modify a verb, an adjective, or another adverb. Adverb clauses act just like adverbs.

> *If you come early,* we can study together. (modifies verb)
>
> I am happy *that you won the prize.* (modifies adjective)
>
> She studies hard *so that she can win a scholarship to college.* (modifies adverb)

Now, write a sentence on the board:

> My brother walked to school this morning.

This is an independent clause, or a complete sentence. Ask students: When I add the word *after*, what happens? The independent clause becomes dependent. The word I added is called a subordinate conjunction. *Subordinate* means *under* or *dependent.*

> After my brother walked to school this morning, he met his friends in the cafeteria.

Now the subordinate conjunction shows the relationship of the idea in the dependent clause to the idea in the independent clause. *That* is not a part of the dependent clause; it is added to the complete clause.

Put similar examples on the board.

Now turn to the workbook and go over subordinate conjunctions, especially the compound subordinate conjunction. Do **Exercise 20** orally to review this concept.

Periodic and loose sentences are important for punctuation. In writing, students can use either kind. Periodic sentences, however, are often used to emphasize the main idea.

> If you want to be popular, if you want to have success, if you want others to respect you, *then buy this product.*

Exercise 24 is an excellent drill for combining sentences using adverb clauses. It also makes a good homework assignment.

Verb sequence is introduced here, relative to the use of the past perfect tense. Do not stay too long on this concept, because students will come to an understanding later when it is necessary for them.

Elliptical adverbial clauses are important especially for correct usage. Do exercises orally first. It is important that students write out the complete elliptical clause. Frequent drills also are important.

Subordination

Teaching students the importance of subordination will help them to develop their writing skills. As they grasp this concept, their writing will mature. Students tend to use the compound sentence. Frequently give them short sentences to combine.

> The street was dark and narrow. We walked slowly and cautiously.
>
> Because the street was dark and narrow, we walked slowly and cautiously. (periodic)

Test

Level 2—Unit 2
Adverb Clauses

Test

Level 2—Unit 2
Adverb Clauses

Name ____________________

Date ____________________

Part A.

Directions: Write the subordinating conjunction on the line.

____________ 1. If you join forces with the debating team, we will be victorious.

____________ 2. While working on my computer last night, I discovered a disk error.

____________ 3. She is a better volleyball player than Tom.

____________ 4. Drive carefully if you don't want to have an accident.

____________ 5. Put the paper on my desk after you finish the last paragraph.

____________ 6. Because he could not adapt to the conditions in the city, he moved to the country.

____________ 7. He was a fast driver even though he was a slow thinker.

____________ 8. You must finish your project today if you want credit for your work.

____________ 9. Our team will win if each member gives over 100 percent.

____________ 10. He worked twelve hours yesterday so that he could be free today.

____________ 11. You can go to camp this summer if you earn the money.

____________ 12. Jane practices swimming six hours a day so that she can qualify for the Olympics.

____________ 13. He enjoys working for my father when my father is out of town.

____________ 14. I cannot go where he wants to send me.

____________ 15. Because the woman was a kleptomaniac, she had to be watched constantly on her shopping trips.

____________ 16. If you suffer from claustrophobia, stay out of close quarters.

____________ 17. My brother is a better tennis player than my sister.

____________ 18. While vacationing in Japan, I became very ill.

____________ 19. When you go to the library, please take my books with you.

____________ 20. Although Bob is a good swimmer, he is really afraid of water.

Part B.

Directions: Make the following independent clauses dependent by adding a subordinate conjunction. Write the conjunction on the line.

____________21. My brother joined the football team last September.

____________22. He worked his way through college.

____________23. Tom worked eight hours last Saturday.

____________24. Jerry wants to go to Paris this summer.

____________25. Pete closed the door with a bang.

____________26. My mother is very careful about germs.

____________27. Mary fears an intruder.

____________28. Save all your canceled stamps.

____________29. We enjoyed the party very much.

____________30. We won the basketball game easily.

Part C.

Directions: Write the letter of the correct answer.

___ 31. John runs faster than (A. he B. him).

___ 32. Bob likes fishing more than (A. I B. me).

___ 33. Arthur enjoys swimming more than (A. he B. him).

___ 34. Jill needed more help than (A. I B. me).

___ 35. The teacher likes historical novels better than (A. he B. him).

___ 36. Bob runs faster than (A. we B. us).

___ 37. Elise is a much better writer than (A. I B. me).

___ 38. Mary is more optimistic than (A. he B. him).

___ 39. Our football team is better than (A. they B. theirs).

___ 40. Jean paints better than (A. him B. he).

Part D.

Directions: Write *P* for periodic or *L* for loose.

___ 41. Although I was finished first, I could not leave.

___ 42. Everyone enjoyed the concert even though it started late.

___ 43. Open the door if you want help.

___ 44. Since you sent her flowers, she has never been the same.

___ 45. You can go to the movie provided you finish your homework.

Unit 3 Adjective Clauses

Objective

Pages 35–49; Exercises 30–43

- To understand adjective clauses and their importance in writing

Relative or adjective clauses are modifiers, limiting a noun or a pronoun. Discuss the workbook explanation. Be sure that students understand the *functions* and *case* of relative pronouns.

Discuss with students the difference between relative and adverb clauses. Emphasize that a subordinate conjunction is never a part of the adverb clause, and that the relative pronoun is always a part of its clause. Work **Exercises 32** and **33** first orally and then in small groups.

Relative adverbs are not very important because they have no function in writing. Go over the explanation and exercise in the workbook so that students have heard of relative adverbs, but do not dwell too long on this concept.

Nonrestrictive and restrictive adjective clauses are often difficult for students to understand. Be sure they know the meaning of the words before writing in the workbook. First, write words like the following on the blackboard:

school	park	saxophone
Joseph	soccer	Doctor Margolis

Ask students: Which words refer to a particular person, place, or thing? Which words do not?

When a relative clause modifies a word that is already restricted, then the clause is not necessary to restrict and commas are required. This clause does not answer the question *which one.* If the noun is not restricted, then the clause is essential and commas are necessary.

Discuss the explanation in the workbook. Do **Exercise 36** with the class. Students in their writing must determine whether a word or clause is essential or not. **Exercises 37–42** give students a feeling of confidence in making decisions of this nature.

Because participles and nouns in apposition also modify restricted or nonrestricted nouns, the workbook explanation and **Exercise 38** focus on this concept. **Exercise 39** gives students practice in combining sentences using relative clauses.

Modification

Words, phrases, and clauses that limit nouns are called modifiers. Go over the workbook explanation that reviews this important concept. **Exercise 43** is a drill on combining sentences using modification. Students might need help at first because there are many ways to combine sentences using modification. They could do each sentence on the board and then do them again for homework. Correcting sentences in groups helps to reinforce the concept.

Test

Level 2—Unit 3
Adjective Clauses
Units 2 and 3 should be completed by the end of the second quarter. If you are ahead of schedule, drill the material rather than start a new unit.

Test
Level 2—Unit 3
Adjective Clauses

Name ____________________

Date ____________________

Part A.

Directions: Write the relative pronoun on the line and underline the antecedent.

____________ 1. Books and magazines that entertain and inform make excellent reading material.

____________ 2. Jane enjoys books that have lots of pictures.

____________ 3. Many people enjoy movies that have substantial plots.

____________ 4. My brother wanted a job that promised good retirement and benefits.

____________ 5. The men and women who enjoy both work and play usually have a fulfilling life.

____________ 6. Last week I visited the Huntington Library that specializes in works of art.

____________ 7. Bob, my cousin, earned a trip to the Bahamas where he will relax for two weeks.

____________ 8. The trip that I planned to take has been canceled.

____________ 9. In England, we visited the house where Shakespeare lived.

____________ 10. Robin Cook, whose books I enjoy, writes real mystery thrillers.

____________ 11. My mother, who loves fishing, went deep-sea fishing yesterday and caught five salmon.

____________ 12. The boat that my father bought is only a small motor-boat.

____________ 13. The work in which Mr. Jones is involved is both strenuous and stressful.

____________ 14. People who enjoy teaching look on students as individuals, not commodities.

____________ 15. Jane, who has taught for the past thirty years, received a Best Teacher Award last month.

____________ 16. People who live in glass houses should not throw stones.

____________ 17. Menial jobs that have no intellectual stimuli often cause stress for college graduates.

____________ 18. John, who has been crippled from birth, received his master's degree from Washington University last week.

____________ 19. The news that was in the newspaper yesterday startled me.

____________ 20. The animal show that I sponsored was a great success.

Part B.

Directions: Write *R* for restrictive clauses or *N* for nonrestrictive clauses.

___ 21. All the papers that were collected yesterday have been burned.

___ 22. The term paper that I handed in last month received an A.

___ 23. The typewriter that is stored in our attic is a real antique.

___ 24. My computer that I received for my birthday is now my most prized possession.

___ 25. Her cat Sammy that she purchased from me last year seems to be very intelligent.

___ 26. Everything that was lying on the floor has been confiscated.

___ 27. We were introduced to Professor Kirchbaum who is a psychology teacher.

___ 28. Did you meet Jerry who is the best basketball player on the team?

___ 29. We saw our oldest brother who is in the army at the mall.

___ 30. The news that was on the board caused much consternation.

___ 31. The earthquake that struck Big Bear caused much damage.

___ 32. The desk that was repaired is now beautiful.

___ 33. My mother whose entire life has been dedicated to serving the poor received a special award last week.

___ 34. The books that we purchased last week have been delivered.

___ 35. None of the materials that we purchased yesterday can be used.

___ 36. I met the man who sent me the books.

___ 37. The cheerleader who won the trophy is going to Washington.

___ 38. Shelly Trigers who is the champion tennis player in our school will represent us in the tournament in New York.

___ 39. We met the woman whose essay won first prize.

___ 40. Sally Jones who is planning to attend Notre Dame will major in journalism.

Unit 4

Noun Clauses

Objectives

- To understand noun clauses and their functions
- To understand the rules governing direct discourse

Pages 50–71; Exercises 44–63

Be sure students understand that the introductory words in noun clauses are not always functional.

Put a few examples on the board:

That John was unhappy was evident.

In this sentence, *that* is not functional. Ask students why.

Where he went is not known.

Where is functional. Why?

Exercise 44 can also be used to drill this concept by asking students how the introductory words are used. Noun clauses have the same uses as a noun, only now the entire clause is used as a subject, direct object, etc. This study is a good review of case.

The difficulty students often have with noun clauses is that the independent clause does not seem complete. Explain that the noun clause always completes the main clause:

That he could not go to school pleased Bob.

In this sentence the subject, the noun clause, completes the predicate.

In **Exercise** 45, all the main clauses are predicated. Students complete the main clauses by adding subjects. The explanations and the exercises drilling the functions of noun clauses should be adequate.

The explanation for the use of *that* in adverb, adjective, and noun clauses should be drilled because this word often poses difficulties. Asking students to write original sentences using *that* in the three dependent clauses will help.

Students often find difficulty in distinguishing between noun clauses in apposition and adjective clauses. Explain that the word *that* in a noun clause is never functional; in an adjective clause it is always functional. The noun clause always answers *what*; the adjective clause answers *where* or *which.*

I read the news that the plane crashed. (noun clause)

I read the news that was in the paper. (adjective clause)

I read the news that she sent to me. (adjective clause)

The workbook's explanation of dependent clauses is a good review. Use **Exercise** 52 to evaluate the students' understanding of this material.

Use **Exercise** 55 to drill for mastery. Students can also add independent clauses to complete the sentences.

The study of *who* and *whom* is always difficult for students. Do **Exercise** 56 orally and then in groups. **Exercise** 57 is a good quiz for evaluative purposes.

Indirect and Direct Discourse

The workbook gives all the rules for direct discourse. Teach one rule at a time. Have students read the answers to the exercises orally, putting in all punctuation.

Optional Assignments

1. Students could imitate **Exercise 62** by writing an original conversation between two different types of people. This is a fun exercise. Have students read their original compositions in groups, and then the best ones to the class.
2. Find a short section from a novel or story that has conversation (for example "The First Seven Years" by Bernard Malamud). Short excerpts review punctuation and lead to good discussions about what the conversation reveals about the speakers.

Test

Level 2—Unit 4
Noun Clauses

Test

Level 2—Unit 4 Noun Clauses

Name ____________________

Date ____________________

Part A.

Directions: Write *S* for subject, *DO* for direct object, *IO* for indirect object, *OP* for object of preposition, *SC* for subject complement, or *A* for apposition.

___ 1. That she was impossible to please was a serious problem.

___ 2. We did not know where she put all our papers.

___ 3. The teacher said that we should relax this weekend.

___ 4. Please give this note to whoever answers the door.

___ 5. The truth of the matter is that she does not know the material.

___ 6. Please give this box to whoever is in the room.

___ 7. We have no opinion about where she should study.

___ 8. That he made a good president is debatable.

___ 9. Whoever needs help, please ask.

___ 10. We agreed that we would meet in the gym.

___ 11. The president mailed his report that he would have to lay off a thousand employees.

___ 12. Please give whomever you meet at the office this letter.

___ 13. The article that the U.S. economy must meet the needs of the American people was published in the *Times*.

___ 14. Lori said that she will graduate from Oberlin in a year.

___ 15. We would like to know about when he actually took the exam.

___ 16. That Lois is a good basketball player cannot be denied.

___ 17. The fact is that Lois will receive a scholarship to Johns Hopkins.

___ 18. The report that the earthquake registered 7.4 shocked me.

___ 19. He demanded that we explain the accident.

___ 20. Mildred said that she would never watch a boxing match.

___ 21. We sent whoever asked for it a special invitation.

___ 22. Whoever took my screwdriver must return it immediately.

___ 23. The fact that she is a good writer is known to everyone.

___ 24. We agreed that Tom should represent the school.

___ 25. His mother said that he could play football in the fall.

Part B.

Directions: Write the letter of the correct answer on the line.

___ 26. (A. Who B. Whom) will be going to the dance?

___ 27. She was speaking about (A. who B. whom)?

___ 28. Please let us know (A. who B. whom) is going.

___ 29. (A. Who B. Whom) do you suppose will be mailing us the list of names and addresses?

___ 30. We did not know (A. who B. whom) to believe.

___ 31. (A. Whoever B. Whomever) plans to go, please let us know.

___ 32. The story was about (A. who B. whom)?

___ 33. To (A. who B. whom) did they give the prize?

___ 34. They will give the prize to (A. whoever B. whomever) gives the best interpretation of the character.

___ 35. (A. Who B. Whom) sent you that package?

Part C.

Directions: Rewrite the following sentences in the space provided and punctuate them correctly.

36. Tom asked where did you put my sweater

37. Everyone who comes early the teacher said will have the best seats

38. Have you read the one-act play Trifles

39. Where are the basketballs the coach yelled.

40. I think it has vanished I said

Unit 5

Compound Sentences

Objectives

- To understand coordination and its uses in writing
- To gain a thorough understanding of a sentence structure

Pages 72–88; Exercises 64–78

Teach the meaning of the compound sentence. Explain that the independent clauses in these sentences cannot be made dependent.

A sentence is a good compound sentence when independent clauses cannot be subordinated.

His name was Alan, and he was the only son of Senator Burk.

The independent clauses in this sentence are equal; each clause is independent of the other. No subordinate conjunction is possible without changing the meaning.

The study of coordination, as opposed to subordination, comes in this section because it reviews all coordination: words, phrases, and clauses.

Coordinate conjunctions never subordinate; they link independent clauses. Students should memorize coordinate conjunctions.

Errors often made in the use of compound sentences are described in the workbook. It is important for students to understand that generally they should subordinate. The examples illustrate errors in coordination. Go over these with the class.

Conjunctive adverbs are often used in writing. Students must realize that they do not join independent clauses; they are generally used transitionally.

Punctuation of compound sentences is explained in the workbook. **Exercise 65** asks students to write original sentences using conjunctive adverbs. Students might do this exercise in class and then put their sentences on the board for correction.

The *comma splice* is inserted here because this is a common student error when writing compound sentences. All the examples in **Exercise 67** are taken from errors made by students. Have students correct in class or for homework.

Correlative conjunctions can easily be used incorrectly. Students should know that correlatives must be used in pairs: neither/nor, either/or. Study the workbook explanation. Work **Exercise 68** orally. The sentences are correct, but students should explain why.

Exercise 69 is a good exercise to do first for homework and then in groups. **Exercise 71** is an original paragraph by a student. It could be punctuated either in class for a quiz or for a homework assignment.

Sentence Function is a review. Most students understand the function of a sentence from grade school. A short review should be sufficient.

Sentence Structure focuses on the four basic types of sentences, giving students a summary view of each type.

Optional Assignment

To drill sentence structure, students should write out a paragraph from a story or novel, or a paragraph can be given to them (for example, "A Worn Path" by Eudora Welty).

Ask students: How many sentences are simple? Which sentences are complex? Are there any other kinds of structure? Can you comment on the paragraph?

Test

Level 2—Unit 5
Compound Sentences

Test

Level 2—Unit 5 Compound Sentences

Name ____________________

Date____________________

Part A.

Directions: Indicate whether the following sentences are *S*, simple; *CX*, complex; *CD*, compound; or *CC*, compound-complex.

___ 1. Gather all the material before you start to write your paper.

___ 2. A person who wishes to succeed must work hard.

___ 3. Meg is a great skater; moreover, she is also a great gymnast.

___ 4. I couldn't write the paper, nor could I find anyone to help me.

___ 5. We planned to be at Shakey's at 1:00 P.M., but an accident that occurred at Tenth Street held us up for two hours.

___ 6. His head bowed in shame, Al quietly left the room.

___ 7. Ted had a strong will and a good personality; when he was challenged by his peers to fight, he positively refused.

___ 8. The game was very close, but Fred, who has a temper, elbowed his opponent, received a technical foul, and thereby lost the game.

___ 9. My sister wants to specialize in science and math in college.

___ 10. We need a date for our prom, or we will have to cancel it.

___ 11. There will be some discomfort on our camping trip, but the fun will far outweigh the inconveniences.

___ 12. The traveler who was evidently in great distress asked us for directions to Santa Monica.

___ 13. Come quickly and quietly.

___ 14. Mrs. Queens, an old friend of my father, loved to take pictures; she carried her camera with her wherever she went.

___ 15. When the weather clears, we will begin our safari.

___ 16. We can't play the game today; it is still raining.

___ 17. Please sign your name on each sheet of paper; otherwise, one of your papers could get lost or misplaced.

___ 18. Peter became class president; Maria, vice president; Margaret, secretary; and Tim, treasurer.

___ 19. Beth swept the floor, dusted the furniture, and vacuumed the bedrooms.

___ 20. She asked, "Where were you last night?"

Part B.

Directions: Underline the parallel items and write the correlatives on the line.

____________ 21. Neither Lois nor Jane will be present for the concert.

____________ 22. Whether my brother or my sister will go is still not settled.

____________ 23. Either you take out the trash or do the dishes.

____________ 24. John is not only a good student but also a good athlete.

____________ 25. Either Molly is stupid or she is very wise.

____________ 26. The old man owned neither a car nor a television.

____________ 27. Both my parents and my sister will attend the school play.

____________ 28. Either Larry does the term paper or he will receive a D.

____________ 29. We did not know whether Tom or Barbara had taken the book.

____________ 30. The coach approved neither his attitude nor his record.

Part C.

Directions: Punctuate the following sentences correctly.

31. If you intend to send the card tomorrow let me sign it first.

32. Her attitude in class caused problems consequently she had to leave.

33. Jack wants to go to Hawaii Mary to Alaska and Joe to Cuba.

34. My watch which is very valuable was stolen last night.

35. Last night there was a severe storm the airport was closed until morning.

36. His speech had many good points but it also caused controversy.

37. We knew that Joe was not ready for the Olympics however he was determined to go.

38. Marilyn who is a great volleyball player received a scholarship to Cal Poly.

39. Buy the necklace it is a great bargain.

40. I work at Ralphs in addition I write articles for the school paper.

41. I did not want to cook moreover we had no food in the house.

42. The race was long and tedious however we won.

43. The earthquake struck at 11:00 P.M. but no one was hurt.

44. She missed the bus for school therefore she had to walk.

45. My car broke down consequently my father had to come after me.

Unit 6

Mood, Potential, Parallelism, Transitions

Objectives

- To understand the subjunctive mood and its uses
- To realize that parallel structure, clear transitions, and references are essential in writing

Pages 89–122; Exercises 79–98

The study of mood and the potential form of the verb is placed in this unit because a knowledge of complex structure is necessary for teaching these concepts.

The indicative and imperative mood should be reviewed briefly. The subjunctive mood is generally a new concept. First explain the meaning of the word *subjunctive.* Then discuss the workbook explanation and work **Exercises 79** and **80**.

Potential form of verbs gives rules for correct usage. The most important one is do not use the potential form with a conditional clause.

If you would have left early, you would have seen me.

It should be written, *If you had left early.* Explain rules 2 and 3 briefly; these rules are often ignored in standard English.

Parallel structure has been stressed throughout Level 2, and its use is very important in writing. Before introducing parallelism, ask students what they have understood about parallel structure during the past three quarters. The workbook explanation and exercises are sufficient at this time. Mastery comes as students use parallel structure.

All the material and exercises in the rest of the workbook are geared to help students improve their sentence structure. Their knowledge of grammar should now be adequate to help them develop their writing skills.

Italics summarizes the rules for the use of italics. This page is a good point of reference when necessary.

Troublesome Word Usage should be studied throughout the year and drilled periodically. Focus on the words that are frequently misused.

Unit 6 completes the material for Level 2. Keep drilling material whenever you see it is needed. Give short quizzes for correct usage. Put two or three incorrect sentences on the board each day to drill a particular concept.

Use Review Tests 1 and 2 more than once. The review helps students spot errors.

Continue periodically to have students find paragraphs from stories or novels. Ask them to give the sentence structure. Study the punctuation and discuss meaning. These excerpts are a tremendous help for students to note the different styles of authors, their points of view, and their attitudes toward the material.

Test

Level 2—Unit 6
Mood, Potential, Parallelism, Transitions

Test

Level 2—Unit 6 Mood, Potential, Parallelism, Transitions

Name ____________________

Date ____________________

Part A.

Directions: Write the letter of the correct word on the line.

___ 1. She wishes that she (A. was B. were) more intelligent.

___ 2. If I (A. was B. were) stronger, I would not be afraid.

___ 3. I suggest that Joe (A. does B. do) his homework.

___ 4. She talked to him as if he (A. was B. were) a child.

___ 5. If I (A. were B. was) able to help you, I would do it.

___ 6. Mr. Peterson prefers that his son (A. go B. goes) to a military school.

___ 7. My mother suggested that Peter (A. stay B. stays) with us for a while.

___ 8. I prefer that he (A. sit B. sits) in the front row.

___ 9. If I (A. were B. was) your mother, you would never talk like that.

___ 10. Bob walks as if he (A. was B. were) injured in the game.

___ 11. The principal demanded that he (A. stays B. stay) after school.

___ 12. The teacher asked that everyone (A. be B. is) silent during the movie.

___ 13. The coach insists that Joe (A. attend B. attends) each practice.

___ 14. I pray that God (A. bless B. blesses) you.

___ 15. The judge ordered that the man (A. stand B. stands) trial.

Part B.

Directions: Correct faulty parallelism in the following sentences.

16. You can invite classmates who are with you in school and your friends from the softball team.

17. The teacher says that I have a strong voice but I sing off key.

18. Our dog ran through our yard, over our fence, and then he came home.

19. My father became tired after he swept the porch, cleaned the garage, then he took his daughter to school.

20. I have poor handwriting more because I am careless than that I have never been taught.

21. Pat not only is a strong student but also a leader.

22. As we entered the gymnasium, you could hear loud cheering.

23. I wrote a good article for the school paper, but it was turned down by the editor.

24. Tom plays neither football or basketball.

25. The sophomores decorated the gym, but it was not appreciated by the juniors.

26. Barbara wrote a beautiful poem but it was laughed at by her classmates.

27. His ability in math is as good if not better than mine.

28. I prefer reading than to go to dances.

29. We decided to go to Magic Mountain and enjoying the rides.

30. I like giving speeches as much as writing a story thrills my sister.

Part C.

Directions: If the sentence is correct, write *C*; if it is incorrect, write *I*.

___ 31. Have you ever read the novel "The Jungle"?

___ 32. My brother loves to watch *Ally McBeal* on TV.

___ 33. We subscribe to "Ladies Home Journal."

___ 34. Her *savoir-faire* made her look confident.

___ 35. I only took one dancing lesson.

___ 36. The comedian proved versatile, inventive, and humorous.

___ 37. We have things to do, people to see, and places that should be visited.

___ 38. To get a job, the application must be sent in today.

___ 39. Playing cards all afternoon, my homework was not finished.

___ 40. Shoes must be worn while eating in that restaurant.

___ 41. Cutting out all wordiness, I improved my composition.

___ 42. Hobbling across the street, my cane slipped from my grasp.

___ 43. When my dog came to the door, we let him in.

___ 44. Albert could neither read or write.

___ 45. If you would have been there, you could have told me then.

Final Examination

Name ____________________

Date ____________________

Part A.

Directions: In each sentence below, identify the incorrect grammatical element and write the letter of that element in the blank provided. If there is no error, write *E.*

____ 1. The summer residents of Luzerne, <u>they</u> (A) told the supervisor to <u>let</u> (B) matters <u>lie</u> (C) just <u>as</u> (D) they are for the time being.

____ 2. The contention <u>is</u> (A) that clothes <u>do</u> (B) not make the man, <u>consequently,</u> (C) I do not see how you <u>can</u> (D) convince him to buy that new suit.

____ 3. <u>Everyone</u> (A) agreed that it was <u>alright</u> (B) to call the meeting for Thursday because there <u>would be</u> (C) no conflict <u>at</u> (D) that time.

____ 4. If they <u>would have listened</u> (A), he <u>was prepared</u> (B) to show <u>them</u> (C) the film after the assembly <u>on Monday.</u> (D)

____ 5. Since one of the teachers <u>has objected</u> (A) to <u>him</u> (B) having the <u>main role</u> (C) in the school play, we had to make a <u>last-minute</u> (D) adjustment.

Part B.

Directions: Write the letter of the correct answer on the line.

___ 6. Everyone thought the best student would be (A. he B. him).

___ 7. How did that medicine (A. affect B. effect) your appetite?

___ 8. About (A. who B. whom) were they speaking?

___ 9. It must have been (A. he B. him) who called.

___ 10. She is (A. sure B. surely) a good loser.

___ 11. This board feels very (A. smooth B. smoothly).

___ 12. (A. Who B. Whom) do you think will be elected president of A.S.B.?

___ 13. The coach thought the next in line to be (A. he B. him).

___ 14. Tom is one of the basketball players who (A. is B. are) going to play in this summer's league.

___ 15. The number of accidents last week (A. was B. were) greater than ever before.

___ 16. Of the two winners in the essay contest, Ed is the (A. better B. best).

___ 17. Neither Pete nor his sisters (A. have B. has) gone to college.

___ 18. Not one of the examples on either test (A. was B. were) answered correctly.

___ 19. A number of desks (A. was B. were) shipped to another school.

___ 20. We all owe a vote of thanks to (A. whoever B. whomever) made this news public.

___ 21. How many of you heard of (A. they B. their C. they're) winning the trophy?

___ 22. What was the (A. effect B. affect) of his talk on the audience?

___ 23. She (A. lay B. lays) the rules on the table.

___ 24. The best player would have to be (A. she B. her).

___ 25. Let's you and (A. I B. me) enter the beauty contest.

___ 26. (A. Who B. Whom) do you suppose they will choose?

___ 27. Everyone wants (A. he B. him) to enter the essay contest.

___ 28. Tom was (A. lying B. laying) beside the fire.

___ 29. (A. Bring B. Take) this material to your art teacher and ask for her advice.

___ 30. Mr. Bob Jones was an (A. eminent B. imminent) lawyer.

Answers to Workbook Exercises Level 2

Unit 1

Exercise 1

1. T	6. L	11. I	16. L
2. L	7. I	12. L	17. I
3. T	8. T	13. T	18. T
4. T	9. I	14. I	19. I
5. I	10. L	15. L	20. T

Exercise 2

1. The wind blew off our roof.	*wind blew roof*
2. Jim, the captain of the basketball team, will represent the team at the meeting.	*Jim (captain) will represent team*
3. The coach took his football team to the USC game.	*coach took team*
4. Jim should have been our first choice for captain.	*Jim should have been choice*
5. We visited Mr. Stafford, president of our Booster Club.	*we visited Mr. Stafford (president)*
6. The salesman sold me a fantastic stereo.	*salesman sold stereo*
7. My mother's pie crusts are always light and flaky.	*crusts are light, flaky*
8. The students entered the auditorium and sat down quietly.	*students entered auditorium and sat*
9. We received very little information about the accident.	*we received information*
10. We greeted the President in Washington, D.C.	*we greeted President*

Exercise 3

1. B	7. B	13. A	19. B
2. A	8. B	14. A	20. B
3. A	9. A	15. A	21. A
4. B	10. A	16. A	22. A
5. B	11. A	17. B	23. A
6. A	12. B	18. A	24. B

25. A	28. A	31. A	34. A
26. A	29. A	32. B	35. B
27. A	30. A	33. B	

Exercise 4

1. A—N	8. B—O	15. A—N	22. A—P
2. A—N	9. A—N	16. B—O	23. B—O
3. A—N	10. B—O	17. B—P	24. A—N
4. B—O	11. B—O	18. B—P	25. A—P
5. B—O	12. B—P	19. B—O	
6. B—O	13. A—P	20. B—O	
7. B—P	14. B—P	21. A—N	

Exercise 5

Part A.

Prepositions will vary, but should be in the following cases.

1. Nominative	4. Possessive	7. Objective	10. Nominative
2. Possessive	5. Nominative	8. Objective	
3. Objective	6. Objective	9. Possessive	

Part B.

11. who	14. whom	17. who	20. who
12. whom	15. whom	18. whom	
13. who	16. whom	19. who	

Exercise 6

Part A.

1. A	4. B	7. A	10. A
2. B	5. A	8. B	
3. B	6. A	9. A	

Part B.

11. The teacher wants Bob and *me* to enter the speech contest next month.
12. The best tennis player is *you.*
13. He injured himself in the game last night. *Correct*
14. Neither Bob nor *I* want to go to the tournament.
15. Either John or *I* will host the party.
16. I did it myself. *Correct*
17. She gave Paul and *me* the good news.
18. I myself will take care of cleaning up after the party. *Correct*
19. You should learn to take the pictures yourself. *Correct*
20. Jason and *I* will present the problem to the faculty members for a solution.

Exercise 7

Part A.

1. P	10. I	19. I	28. P
2. I	11. G	20. G	29. I
3. G	12. P	21. P	30. I
4. G	13. P	22. P	31. I
5. G	14. I	23. P	32. G
6. I	15. G	24. G	33. P
7. I	16. I	25. I	34. G
8. I	17. G	26. G	35. G
9. I	18. G	27. G	

Part B.

36. G	39. G	42. G	45. G
37. P	40. P	43. G	
38. G	41. P	44. P	

Exercise 8

1. preposition	8. verb	15. gerund	22. participle
2. apposition	9. infinitive	16. gerund	23. preposition
3. verb	10. infinitive	17. infinitive	24. apposition
4. preposition	11. apposition	18. apposition	25. gerund
5. gerund	12. preposition	19. infinitive	
6. infinitive	13. infinitive	20. gerund	
7. gerund	14. apposition	21. preposition	

Exercise 9

Original sentences

Exercise 10

1. C	6. M	11. C	16. C
2. C	7. M	12. M	17. C
3. M	8. C	13. C	18. C
4. C	9. C	14. M	19. C
5. C	10. M	15. M	20. M

Exercise 11

1. company made Clarence chief
2. Bob, Carol made house comfortable
3. she painted garage purple
4. Jean called brother nuisance
5. you consider proposition open
6. principal made Gina chairperson
7. stylist made hair curly
8. school chose Jody queen

9. mother named brother Ted
10. president appointed friend director

Exercise 12

1. O	8. O	15. S	22. S
2. D	9. S	16. D	23. D
3. O	10. O	17. S	24. O
4. D	11. D	18. O	25. O
5. S	12. S	19. S	
6. S	13. O	20. D	
7. D	14. O	21. D	

Exercise 13

1. A	8. A	15. A	22. A
2. A	9. B	16. B	23. A
3. B	10. A	17. B	24. B
4. B	11. B	18. A	25. B
5. A	12. A	19. A	
6. B	13. B	20. B	
7. A	14. B	21. B	

Exercise 14

Original sentences

Exercise 15

Original sentences

Unit 2

Exercise 16

1. P	4. C	7. C	10. C
2. P	5. P	8. P	
3. C	6. C	9. C	

Exercise 17

Original sentences

Exercise 18

1. participle	5. infinitive
2. adjective	6. gerund
3. participle	7. verb
4. preposition	8. gerund

Exercise 19

1. I	6. I	11. I	16. I
2. C	7. C	12. I	17. C
3. C	8. C	13. I	18. C
4. I	9. C	14. I	19. C
5. I	10. I	15. I	20. I

Exercise 20

Answers may vary.

Exercise 21

Answers may vary.

Exercise 22

1. unless	5. if	9. because	13. than
2. provided	6. when	10. so that	14. even though
3. where	7. because	11. since	15. whenever
4. when	8. when	12. if	

Exercise 23

1. My mother telephoned me <u>before</u> she left for Canada. *L*
2. <u>If</u> you call before ten o'clock, leave a message. *P*
3. She remained in the room <u>until</u> I had finished the essay. *L*
4. <u>Although</u> Bob is a good writer, he often makes careless mistakes. *P*
5. Check over your examination paper <u>before</u> you hand it in. *L*
6. <u>Unless</u> you make a different choice, I will not sponsor you. *P*
7. <u>Because</u> she is stubborn and because she will not listen to others, she often causes untold difficulties. *P*
8. You can go <u>provided</u> you are home by 1:00 A.M. *L*
9. <u>Although</u> it was still early, we decided to leave. *P*
10. You will have no friends <u>as</u> <u>long</u> <u>as</u> you have that negative attitude. *L*
11. <u>If</u> you make the team, you must be willing to practice every day. *P*
12. Did you meet Tom, my cousin, <u>when</u> you were in San Diego? *L*
13. I will go with you <u>as</u> <u>soon</u> <u>as</u> I get my sweater. *L*
14. <u>Because</u> Jan won the nomination, we were all delighted. *P*
15. We left early <u>in</u> <u>order</u> <u>to</u> get good seats. *L*

Exercise 24

Answers may vary.

Exercise 25

1. studied A took B
2. gathered A wrote B
3. graduated B worked A
4. returned A called B
5. stole A left B
6. sneezed, coughed A moved B
7. wrote A be prosecuted B
8. went B joined A
9. made A won B
10. asked A accepted B

Exercise 26

1. Tim enjoys football more than I *enjoy football.*
2. Alice works as hard as Mary *works.*
3. Barbara likes me better than *she likes* her.
4. Our basketball team is better than theirs *is.* (or *their basketball team is*)
5. Bob runs faster than Jim *runs.*
6. My father likes baseball more than *he likes* soccer.
7. Jean is not as kind as her twin *is kind.*
8. Our math class needed more assistance than his *class needed assistance.*
9. Arthur enjoys typing more than *he enjoys* algebra.
10. John is more pessimistic than I *am.* (or *than I am pessimistic*
11. Jill works harder than she *works hard.*
12. California is larger than Arizona *is large.*
13. I enjoy her concerts more than his *concerts.*
14. Paul is a better pianist than Jeannie *is a pianist.*
15. Jake is as tall as my brother *is tall.*
16. He is wiser than Ted *is wise.*
17. John needs more help than she *needs help.*
18. The teacher likes Joe better than *the teacher likes* me.
19. Bob is better at tennis than she *is.*
20. Jack studies harder than she *studies hard.*

Exercise 27

1. when you are filling in your applications
2. while he was fixing his car
3. when you are planting marigolds
4. than Greg is writer
5. than Carl enjoys swimming
6. than Jerry requires help
7. while she was snorkeling
8. than my father is old
9. than Jim understands math
10. while she was swimming

11. when you are called
12. than Mr. Jones is a math teacher
13. than Ted hits the ball
14. when you are eating lunch
15. than Jill is happy
16. while he is studying for the exam
17. when you are applying for a job
18. when you are handing in your papers
19. than I enjoy taking care of children
20. when you are playing ball
21. than he is tall
22. than I enjoy music lessons
23. than Jack is mature
24. while he was eating lunch
25. when you are playing the piano

Exercise 28

Answers may vary.

Exercise 29

Part A.

1. We were determined to win the tournament so that we could get a computer.
2. Tim studied French every night since he wanted to visit Paris next summer.
3. The entire sophomore class was happy when Bill won the election.
4. John is taller than Fred.
5. Playing basketball, if you have talent, can give you many fringe benefits.
6. We plan to go to Canada this summer because my father's sister lives there.
7. Jean wrote her essay very carefully so that the teacher would enter it into the English contest.
8. Although there were many people auditioning for the play, John easily received a part.
9. Working hard until his project was finished, Bob received an A.
10. (While—understood) Working for my uncle last summer, I earned enough money to buy a car.

Part B.

11. P	14. P	17. L	20. P
12. L	15. P	18. L	
12. P	16. L	19. P	

Part C.

Answers may vary.

Unit 3

Exercise 30

1. A box of oranges that was shipped last week has never arrived. — *box*
2. My sister-in-law, who lives in Florida, will be visiting us next week. — *sister-in-law*
3. We knew the policeman who gave us a ticket. — *policeman*
4. The house that Jack built was destroyed by fire. — *house*
5. Our basketball team, which is still undefeated, will play for the championship next Friday. — *team*
6. My aunt, whose term of office will end in January, plans to live in Paris. — *aunt*
7. The dog that my father gave me for my birthday is now just six months old. — *dog*
8. *A Tale of Two Cities*, which we studied last year, gives a detailed picture of the French Revolution. — *A Tale of Two Cities*
9. He sat on the chair that my brother had just painted. — *chair*
10. My ring that I lost several weeks ago was returned last night. — *ring*

Exercise 31

1. ADV
2. ADV
3. ADJ
4. ADJ
5. ADV
6. ADV
7. ADJ
8. ADJ
9. ADJ
10. ADJ

Exercise 32

1. that S letter
2. whom OP girl
3. which S movie
4. that DO position
5. whose R Borg
6. that DO bicycle
7. that DO photographs
8. that DO video
9. whom DO anyone
10. that DO novel
11. whose R friend
12. whom OP professor
13. that DO novel
14. that DO bracelet
15. who S everyone
16. that DO project
17. that DO book
18. whose R Aunt Jane
19. whom DO relative
20. that S news
21. that DO report
22. which OP bedroom
23. whose R book
24. that DO poem
25. which OP scene

Exercise 33

Answers should be expressed with *that.*

Exercise 34

1. The book I bought for my mother last year is now out of print.
2. The clothes that were shipped to the missions were damaged in transit.
3. We all visited the zoo where we saw many kinds of animals.
4. The flowers that I took to the hospital were for my cousin Joe.
5. The news that was on the radio spoke of a flood in Germany.
6. Did you meet Tom Selleck, who was on the plane with you?
7. I can see no reason why I should go to New York.
8. It was the exact moment when the accident happened.
9. The paint that I needed so desperately never arrived.
10. The prison where he spent the last twenty years burned down.
11. The dog that I received for my birthday is a golden retriever.
12. The box in which I put the jewelry is misplaced.
13. The talk that he gave to his students really motivated them.
14. The announcement that school would close for a week startled everyone.
15. My third quarter report card that the school sent to my parents had three As.

Exercise 35

1. R
2. N
3. R
4. R
5. N
6. R
7. N
8. N
9. R
10. R
11. N
12. R
13. R
14. N
15. R
16. N
17. R
18. R
19. R
20. R

Exercise 36

1. Antecedent is *boy*, nonrestricted. Clause is restrictive. Do not use commas.
2. Antecedent is *kitten*, nonrestricted. Clause is restrictive. Do not use commas.
3. Antecedent is *Tom*, restricted. Clause is nonrestrictive. Use commas: *Tom, who is my best friend, will be moving to Australia.*
4. Antecedent is *Professor Jones*, restricted. Clause is nonrestrictive. Use commas: *Professor Jones, who is an excellent teacher, has been my teacher for two years.*
5. Antecedent is *ring*, nonrestricted. Clause is restrictive. Do not use commas.
6. Antecedent is *book*, nonrestricted. Clause is restrictive. Do not use commas.
7. Antecedent is *essay*, restricted. Clause is nonrestrictive. Use commas: *My essay, which won first prize, will be sent to Washington, D.C.*
8. Antecedent is *papers*, nonrestricted. Clause is restrictive. Do not use commas.
9. Antecedent is *bike*, nonrestricted. Clause is restrictive. Use commas: *Jerry's bike, which was damaged in the accident, has been repaired.*
10. Antecedent is *umbrella*, nonrestricted. Clause is restrictive. Do not use commas.

Exercise 37

If the answer is N, commas are necessary.

1. N	6. R	11. N
2. N	7. N	12. R
3. N	8. R	13. N
4. R	9. N	14. N
5. R	10. R	15. N

Exercise 38

If the answer is N, commas are necessary.

1. R	4. R	7. R	10. N
2. R	5. R	8. N	
3. N	6. R	9. N	

Exercise 39

Answers may vary.

Exercise 40

If the answer is N, commas are necessary.

1. R	6. N	11. R	16. R
2. R	7. N	12. N	17. R
3. R	8. R	13. N	18. N
4. N	9. N	14. R	19. N
5. N	10. R	15. R	20. N

Exercise 41

1. Computers (that have already taken over) in the business world are also now a must in classrooms and libraries.
2. Processing centers will disperse information (that the home computers request).
3. Many schools have added computer programs (that help young people learn).
4. Computers have changed the work habits of people (who work in offices).
5. Many people (whose jobs are in offices) are now starting to work in their homes.
6. Students (who use computers) seem to understand concepts easier.
7. First graders are now using computers (that help them write).
8. My brother has a computer (that helps him with his calculus).
9. Many hospitals today have computers (that detect diseases).
10. My cousin, (who studies medicine), uses a computer daily.

Exercise 42

1. whose R students
2. that DO book
3. whom OP man
4. that S jobs
5. who S father
6. who S people
7. that S studio
8. that S Disneyland

9. that S museum
10. who S Walton
11. that S room
12. that S desks
13. that S room
14. who S man
15. that S boxes
16. that DO computer
17. which DO convertible
18. that S door
19. who S Esther
20. that S skit
21. who S Jody
22. that DO essay
23. that S shop
24. who S Jane
25. who S Stevie

Exercise 43

Answers may vary.

Unit 4

Exercise 44

1. That Steve will succeed in his new job is almost assured.
2. Whoever finishes first will receive a prize.
3. What you do next depends on you.
4. Whatever way you go does not really matter.
5. Whether he will finish on time is debatable.
6. That Jim is a good student is evident by his work.
7. What Elsie did with the prize money was up to her.
8. Whoever finishes first must do the dishes.
9. When the storm will be over is hard to estimate.
10. That John is very clever was shown yesterday.

Exercise 45

Answers may vary.

Exercise 46

1. No one in the class knew where the teacher put our papers. *adverb*
2. The teacher said that we would go on a field trip soon. *no*
3. Mollie said that she would be moving next semester. *no*
4. Bob asked which class would be dropped. *adjective*
5. We did not know how he would react to the announcement. *adverb*
6. We agreed that we would debate the issue tomorrow. *no*
7. The catalog lists which teacher will teach each course. *adjective*
8. We could not remember when the test would be given. *adjective*
9. We all wondered which book we would read next. *adjective*
10. We debated where we would hold the prom. *adverb*

Exercise 47

1. whoever
2. whomever
3. whoever
4. whomever
5. whoever
6. whoever
7. whomever
8. whoever
9. whomever
10. whomever

Exercise 48

1. The rumor was that Joe was leaving the state.
2. My one desire is that I can go to Vassar.
3. The news was that our team had won the game.
4. The truth is that there can be no free day this semester.
5. The fact was that Jim failed both exams.
6. His purpose in holding the meeting was that there could be more group unity.
7. My only reason for my action was that the boys would be more respectful.
8. His desire could be that he wants to be president.
9. Jerry's hope is that he can become a journalist.
10. The news is that school will be closed on Friday.

Exercise 49

1. Just leave the message with whoever answers the door.
2. We argued about where we would eat.
3. They wondered about how they would cross the desert.
4. My friend was angered by whoever rang the doorbell.
5. We are seldom pleased with what they tell us.
6. Jerry had no idea of why he sent that message.
7. Give this pencil to whoever bought it.
8. We were overjoyed by what he told us.
9. These papers are for the work you must do.
10. Send these reports to whoever requested them.

Exercise 50

1. Send whoever asked for it this money.
2. That you can be very slow sometimes is evident.
3. Whoever works the hardest will receive the prize.
4. I cannot understand why he refused to attend the workshops.
5. We all agreed that we would not meet for another month.
6. The argument started over who would take Jerry to school.
7. That we won the game did not surprise us.
8. The question is whether we can play in the tournament.
9. What you choose to do is your decision.
10. The decision that we should all remain in the room angered us.
11. Your grade on the final exam will determine whether you will pass the course.
12. My father's worry, how he can get a job, affected the entire house.
13. We will agree with whoever gives the best advice.
14. The most difficult question was whether the entire time should be devoted to a single topic.
15. They will select whoever puts in an application.
16. She asked whether I would help her write the paper.

17. She said that Jerry and she would leave later.
18. That the paper was poorly written was certainly evident.
19. My brother's favorite excuse is that the dog tore up his homework.
20. That my little sister was selected the best player pleased my father.

Exercise 51

1. N	4. N	7. A	10. A
2. N	5. A	8. N	
3. A	6. N	9. A	

Exercise 52

1. R	9. A	17. A	25. A
2. A	10. A	18. R	26. N
3. R	11. R	19. A	27. R
4. A	12. A	20. R	28. N
5. R	13. A	21. N	29. A
6. N	14. A	22. N	30. R
7. N	15. N	23. N	
8. N	16. A	24. R	

Exercise 53

1. who	11. whom	21. object of the preposition
2. after	12. after	22. direct object
3. that	13. as long as	23. indirect object
4. where	14. while	24. that
5. that	15. direct object	25. before
6. apposition	16. so that	26. direct object
7. subject	17. as if	27. that
8. apposition	18. who	28. apposition
9. than	19. where	29. if
10. since	20. that	30. when

Exercise 54

Original sentences

Exercise 55

1. R	10. R	19. R	28. A
2. A	11. N	20. R	29. A
3. N	12. A	21. R	30. R
4. R	13. R	22. R	31. N
5. A	14. R	23. A	32. N
6. R	15. A	24. N	33. N
7. A	16. N	25. R	34. N
8. N	17. N	26. N	35. R
9. A	18. N	27. R	36. R

37. N	41. A	45. N	49. N
38. N	42. N	46. N	50. N
39. A	43. R	47. N	
40. N	44. A	48. R	

Exercise 56

1. B	10. B	19. A	28. B
2. B	11. A	20. B	29. B
3. B	12. B	21. B	30. B
4. A	13. B	22. B	31. B
5. A	14. B	23. A	32. B
6. A	15. B	24. A	33. A
7. B	16. A	25. A	34. B
8. B	17. A	26. A	35. B
9. A	18. A	27. A	36. A

Exercise 57

1. That she is impossible to please makes it difficult to live with her. *S*
2. We did not know where she put all the papers. *DO*
3. The teacher said that we should relax this weekend. *DO*
4. Please give this note to whoever answers the door. *OP*
5. The truth is that she did not study. *SC*
6. Please give whoever answers the door this note. *IO*
7. We have no idea of why she is moving to Canada. *OP*
8. That he would make a good president is debatable. *S*
9. Whoever needs help on the project should ask me. *S*
10. We agreed that we would all meet in the gym. *DO*
11. His recommendation that we should lay off at least a hundred employees brought us real grief. *A*
12. That this will cause a terrible hardship is inevitable. *S*
13. The article that Japan needs help surprised no one. *A*
14. Lori said that she will graduate from Purdue University in two years. *DO*
15. We would like to know when he took the state boards. *DO*
16. That Lois is a good basketball player cannot be denied. *S*
17. The fact is that Lois will receive a college scholarship. *SC*
18. The report that the earthquake registered 7.4 shocked me. *A*
19. He demanded to know who set off the alarm. *DO*
20. Mildred said that she had never watched a boxing match. *DO*

Exercise 58

1. I asked, "How do you know she will be on time?"
2. The boy cried, "I spent three hours on homework last night."
3. "Why did you leave so quickly?" he asked.
4. "Are you going to ask Ted to the picnic?" Mary asked.

5. "I really like our school jacket," I said.
6. The coach said, "We are coming home the victors on Friday night."
7. "Where are you going this summer?" I asked.
8. "Have you seen that movie before?" James inquired.
9. "You must keep your eye on the ball," the coach instructed.
10. "Don't forget my anniversary," my mother announced one morning.

Exercise 59

1. "It is not true," she replied, "that I did his homework for him."
2. "When you visit me in Texas," my cousin wrote, "be sure to bring your hat and boots."
3. "We will be closing the park for a week," the ranger said, "in order to make the necessary repairs."
4. "I'll have to ask the teacher," Carla answered, "because I can't give you permission to leave."
5. "If we can win this game," Jeff said, "then we can be the champions of Arkansas."
6. "If I can get to the box office this morning," Lori promised, "I'll get the tickets."
7. "When you finish the dishes," my mother said, "you may visit your friend."
8. "After you see the movie," Peter replied, "meet us at Carnation Parlor"
9. "Look up the material in the encyclopedia," the professor said, "if you want to have a documented term paper."
10. "I fail to see," Jason said, "how you wrote that paper so quickly."

Exercise 60

1. "I will never forget," Bob said, "the evening we camped out at Lake Mountains. It was the worst evening of my life."
2. "I wish I had studied harder," Jean moaned. "I know I am going to fail this test."
3. "If you leave immediately," I said, "you will be on time for class. You don't want to be late a third time."
4. "I believe," said Ted, "that we can reach the campsite by 2:00 A.M. We could get there sooner if we would stop dawdling."
5. "Tom," I asked, "may I borrow your book for an hour? I will put it on your desk when I am finished."

Exercise 61

1. "Where did you put the balloons for the party?" I asked.
2. The boy screamed, "The boy in that blue convertible stole my jacket!"
3. Did the speech teacher say, "Meet near the gym at 8:00 A.M."?
4. "Were you planning to leave later?" I asked.
5. "Has everyone bought tickets for the Lakers game Friday night?" he asked.
6. "Did you see my sister in the cafeteria?" I asked.
7. "We were certainly not aware," the cop replied, "that the spring vacation had already started. Give us the exact dates so that we can check."

8. "Are you planning," Sharon asked, "to go to the Friendship Dance on Saturday night? It is sponsored by the freshman class."
9. Did you see his bike at the park?" Paul asked.
10. "Did you read the sign that said, "Boys not allowed"?
11. "Nothing could make her feel better," I said. "She was really upset."
12. My mechanic said, "your engine needs work. You better let us keep your car overnight."
13. My uncle called my house this morning and said, "We have a beautiful baby girl."
14. Did you hear the principal say, "School will be canceled for two days"?
15. The student asked, "Did you see my math book lying around anywhere?"
16. The judge said, "There is a law that says, 'No drunk driving.'"
17. My brother ran into the house and enthusiastically announced, "I made 100% on my semester math exam." (or !")
18. Did you read the notice that said, "If you are going to Europe this summer, please turn in your registration form by Friday of this week"?
19. "The game was really a close one," he said, "It took until the last four seconds to win."
20. Did Miss Jones really say, "I will not accept late papers"?
21. My teacher asked, "Who spilled this ink?"
22. The operator announced, "A world record was set in the last race."
23. If you decide to go with us, please let us know by tomorrow.
24. "Nothing," he said, "atone for the loss of my little brother."
25. Didn't you read the notice that said, "No smoking"?

Exercise 62

New paragraph each time the person speaks.

Exercise 63

Part A.

Original Sentences

Part B.

13. Jerry said, "I am going camping on Saturday. Do you want to come with me?"
14. "Where," she asked, "did you put the paper I gave you to read?"
15. Did you study the one-act play "Trifles"?
16. "While the weather is warm," Joan said, "let's go to the beach. I am dying to feel those fresh sea breezes."
17. "Did you finish your term paper?" I asked. "I stayed up all night to finish mine."
18. Did you hear him say, "There is nothing we can do about the situation"?
19. "Next week," our philosophy teacher said, "we will discuss *Carpe diem*: seize the day."
20. "Out of my way," yelled Melissa. "I'm late!"

Unit 5

Exercise 64

1. consequently
2. moreover
3. therefore
4. likewise
5. similarly

Exercise 65

Original Sentences

Exercise 66

Answers may vary.

Exercise 67

1. Our team played hard; we lost by ten points.
2. I wasn't frightened by the wolf; I was terrified.
3. Order your tickets early; you might not get one.
4. Proceed quickly to the gym; we want to start immediately.
5. Terry wrote several letters to the editor; she never received an answer.
6. I could hardly wait to swim; the water looked so inviting.
7. We were all there for the party; Jack came an hour late.
8. The cookies were in the pantry; nobody looked there.
9. Hurry and greet the visitors; we can't keep them waiting.
10. My car is old; it still runs well.

Exercise 68

1. Bob is (not only) a fine musician (but also) an excellent basketball player.
2. (Either) Jerry finishes his assignment (or) he will fail the course.
3. (Either) I will borrow the book from the library (or) I will buy it.
4. The gymnasium will be used (not only) for athletic events (but also) for dances.
5. (Whether) he stays in school (or) goes to work must be his decision.
6. I approve of (neither) your attitude (nor) your actions.
7. She will probably ask (either) Caroline (or) Michelle to go with her.
8. Jack is (not only) an excellent student (but also) a fine young man.
9. (Either) he is justified by his remarks (or) he is proved guilty.
10. (Both) the principal (and) his secretary will attend the meeting.
11. The old man owned (neither) a coat (nor) a hat.
12. The teacher asked (whether) Jane (or) I had taken her book from her desk.
13. (Both) blue (and) yellow drapes were brought to her room.
14. The accident was blamed (not only) on Bob (but also) on the entire club.
15. (Either) he forged the check (or) he destroyed it.

Exercise 69

1. I enjoy working at the store, skiing at Mammoth, and *practicing* ice skating at our rink.
2. Albert had signed up *for either* AP calculus or physics.

3. I *have neither* the time nor the patience for his continually rude conduct.
4. Joe wants *to be either* a doctor or a veterinarian.
5. He *had neither* eaten nor slept for two days.
6. This problem *should be considered not only* by the president of the firm but also by the vice president.
7. *She is not only* a fantastic swimmer but *also* a fabulous dancer.
8. You must *know not only* how to take pictures but also how to develop them.
9. Everyone admires her courage, but *no one admires her actions.*
10. I *go neither* to the right nor to the left.
11. She is neither very brilliant *nor* very stupid.
12. You can *go either* to the baseball convention or to the basketball convention.
13. You really *ought to either* telephone your mother or stop to see her.
14. You *can get* your tickets *either* in the office or in the gym.
15. I *was neither* upset nor angry with George.

Exercise 70

1. Last night there was a heavy fog; the airport was closed until morning.
2. The population of New Mexico grows each year; everyone loves the climate.
3. Jerry was elected the president of the senior class; Cindy, the vice-president; Lori, the secretary; and Brian, the treasurer.
4. If you enjoy traveling, visit Hong Kong this summer; it will be an unforgettable trip.
5. We all knew that Bill was not well enough to play; however, he was determined to try.
6. Matt Fowler, who is the school's top football player, enjoys soccer as well; he plans to play football next year at the Air Force Academy.
7. Because Martha is interested in the medicine, she plans to major in this field; after college she wants to spend her life helping the sick.
8. Jim wants to be an artist; Bob, an engineer; and Raymond, an elementary school teacher.
9. That the diplomatic service needs a complete revision was Senator Norman's statement; he stressed the need of a committee to study the problem.
10. Try me; you'll soon find out what I can do.
11. My car, which was in the accident last night, is totaled; I hope my insurance will help me buy a new one.
12. Try on this sweater; it is your favorite color.
13. His argument has some merit; however, it goes too far.
14. Among those present were Dr. J. Jones, president of MWC; Albert C. Pyle, superintendent of schools; B. Crawley, manager of the Hilton Hotel; and E. T. Miller, secretary of the Brown Corporation.
15. Although I seldom have trouble with grammar, I have much trouble with punctuation; the rules never seem to be consistent.
16. Carrying more than his share of the load, Bob hurt his back.
17. It was an exercise in patience, but it also became an exercise in endurance.
18. Life, according to the philosopher, is a battle of wits.
19. Seeing her standing by the candy counter, Sam slipped out the back door.
20. I couldn't solve the problem, nor could I find anyone else to help me.

Exercise 71

In *Lord of the Flies* by William Golding, external action reveals the personalities of the main characters. Through their actions and external conflicts, Ralph becomes the voice of reason; Jack, the savagery of man; and Simon, the embodiment of truth. From the beginning of the story, Ralph represents the guidance of civilized reason. Concerned with the common good and with justice, he strives to establish a sense of law and order on the island. Since his main concern is to be rescued, he insists on the signal fire and chides Jack for letting it go out and ruining their chances of getting rescued. This fire becomes a source of conflict, yet Ralph sticks to reason in insisting that it be kept burning. Eventually losing the support of the other boys, Ralph ends up an outcast. While he can see the value of retaining the externals of civilization, the others don't share his adult view and succumb to savagery. Ralph, consequently, becomes the last voice of common sense and values on the island. He never totally abandons society; in the end he weeps for the end of innocence and the darkness in men's hearts.

Exercise 72

1. IN ?	6. D .	11. D .	16. E !
2. IM .	7. IM .	12. E !	17. IN ?
3. IM .	8. IM .	13. D .	18. D .
4. E !	9. IN ?	14. IN ?	19. IN ?
5. IM .	10. E ! E !	15. D .	20. IM.

(In making a request with please, the sentence is usually imperative.)

Exercise 73

1. I never play it/ I love football/ although
2. she was disqualified/ Mary forgot to send in her registration/ because
3. news startled everyone/ he was elected president/ apposition
4. we left/ it started to rain/ when
5. flower died/ that I grew for the contest/ that
6. truth is/ Tom received scholarship/ subject complement
7. we all saw accident/ that happened on 4th Street/ that
8. You do know/ what he said/ direct object
9. (clause as subject) bothered my mother/ I wanted to live with my father/ subject
10. we read news / that was in the paper/ that

Exercise 74

Original Sentences

Exercise 75

1. S	4. CO	7. CO	10. S; COR
2. COR	5. COR	8. CO	
3. S	6. CA	9. CO	

Exercise 76

1. CD	6. CC	11 CD	16. CX
2. S	7. S	12. CC	17. CC
3. CX	8. CC	13. S	18. CX
4. CX	9. S	14. CC	19. CX
5. CD	10. CD	15. CX	20. CC

Exercise 77

1. IM .	4. D .	7. IN ?	10. E !
2. IN ?	5. IM .	8. D .	
3. E !	6. E !	9. IM .	

Exercise 78

1. CX	4. S	7. CD	10. S
2. S	5. CD	8. S	
3. CC	6. CX	9. CC	

Unit 6

Exercise 79

1. were	6. were	11. be	16. were
2. keep	7. remain	12. were	17. take
3. get	8. were	13. were	18. be
4. were	9. be	14. were	19. were
5. keep	10. be	15. were	20. were

Exercise 80

Original sentences

Exercise 81

1. If you would have sent us your resume, we might have hired you. *had*
2. John said that he may go with us to the game on Friday night. *might*
3. If you would have been willing to practice more frequently, you would have been a better skater. *had*
4. Jerry agreed that we may finish our project in time to enter it into the science fair. *might*
5. Mother said that I can go to the show. *could*
6. If you would have attended the meeting, you would have known the major problem. *had*
7. Jeannie's mother said that Jeannie can attend the concert on Friday night. *could*
8. The old lady says that I might help her to weed her lawn on Saturday morning. *may*
9. Margie said that I must take a course in art if I plan to go to college in the fall. *should*
10. The coach said that I can beat Jeff in tennis if I practiced harder. *could*

Exercise 82

1. The entire team ordered hamburgers with cheese and onions, ice cream, and a Diet Pepsi.
2. On our end-of-the-year picnic, our class enjoyed barbecuing hamburgers, hiking through the woods, and playing baseball in the park.
3. The teacher asked us whether we preferred going to Magic Mountain, going swimming at Lake Sherman, or enjoying a Dodger baseball game.

Exercise 83

1. Jean is editor not only of the school paper but also of our yearbook.
2. Paul is either on top of the world or deep in the abyss.
3. Mary is neither a good student nor a good worker.
4. He plays neither football nor basketball.
5. Paul is not only planning not only to be a physician, but also to specialize in pediatrics.

Exercise 84

1. The girls in the class prepared a delicious lunch, but the boys gobbled it down.
2. When you go to your first prom, you want to look your best.
3. The freshmen decorated the gym for the welcome dance, but the seniors criticized the decorations.
4. My sister and I tried out for the school play, and the director chose me for the lead.
5. Joe turned in the best composition, but his friends laughed at it.

Exercise 85

1. I can throw the ball farther than Pete can.
2. Her hair is just like her mother's hair.
3. Jane is as happy, as if not happier, than Michelle.

   or

   Jane is as happy as Michelle, if not happier.
4. His voice is as good as, if not better, than Brian's.

   or

   His voice is as good as Brian's, if not better.
5. Jeff's ability to write was like his brother's.

Exercise 86

1. My brother prefers staying home to going to parties.
2. He was pleased less by the recognition of his abilities than by his accomplishments.
3. By studying for the examination and by not worrying about the results, you will probably be more successful.
4. He was chosen because of his ability rather than because he was a good leader.
5. We all decided to go out for pizza rather than to go to an expensive restaurant.
6. Remember that working hard in high school is commendable, but trying to do too much is foolish.
7. Because Tom was an excellent student, because he was determined and conscientious, and because he wanted to be a doctor, he was given an academic scholarship to Duke University.
8. The class decided to visit the museum and see everything on display.
9. His efforts are as great as, if not greater, than Ted's.

   or

   His efforts are as great as Ted's, if not greater.
10. Mabel will go either to Georgia Tech and study engineering or to Occidental and study music.
11. They discussed firing the manager, hiring a replacement, and changing the pitching staff.
12. At the picnic we played ball in the park while the spectators ate all the lunch.

13. This situation should be considered not only by the coach but also by the players.
14. Jerry built model airplanes because he enjoyed flying and building them.
15. When the bell rang for class, the principal opened the doors.
16. Jack belongs not only to the soccer team but also to the golf team.
17. I play the piano as well as, if not better than, Jean.
    or
    I play the piano as well as Jean, if not better.
18. I enjoy playing the organ, singing in the choir, and organizing concerts.
19. We all gathered in the auditorium to listen to his talk, but several of the students paid little attention.
20. Giving a speech before a large audience can require more courage than taking the SAT.

Exercise 87

Original sentences

Exercise 88

Answers may vary.

Exercise 89

Answers may vary.

Exercise 90

1. Bob likes to swim, play cards, and dance.
2. Liz was as happy as Peggy, if not happier, over the outcome of the debate.
3. Lois was lively, athletic, and likable.
4. The principal informed neither the faculty nor the parents about the outcome of the questionnaire.
5. Playing baseball, Jerry broke the window, and someone replaced it immediately.
6. The baseball team could choose either to go to a baseball game or to go to an amusement park.
7. We bought a board six feet long and two feet wide.
8. Kevin's walk was like a bear's.
9. The weather in Chicago is as cold as, if not colder than, New York.
10. John pitched the first six innings, and Dave pitched the last three.

Exercise 91

Answers may vary.

Exercise 92

Answers may vary.

Exercise 93

1. I read only one novel this summer.
2. To complete my term paper, I need to do some research.
3. While studying computer literacy, I learned new methods for writing papers.
4. John agreed that he would go straight home when the dance was over.
5. When I saw the sunset, I experienced a feeling of awe.
6. Racing hurriedly to get to school on time, I broke my shoelaces.
7. While standing in the ball park, I heard an airplane.
8. Many people asked whether we had extra tickets to the concert.
9. The real reason why he is not playing in the game tonight is that he is suspended for being truant last Friday.
10. We drove in my car to the concert where Jim was scheduled to sing.

Exercise 94

1. He thought we were not ready to handle the project without supervision.
2. The principal thought the freshmen were too immature to sponsor a dance.
3. I am bewildered by the events that took place this evening.
4. Football in colleges should be eliminated because it often causes physical injury.
5. The school should not tolerate tardiness.
6. We did not want to go to the game because it would interfere with an important exam the next day.
7. The boy handing out leaflets before the show hopes to be an actor.
8. Miss Powers, the math teacher, will give help if you ask her.
9. When Bob walked into the gym, the girls crowded around him.
10. Jennifer said that her brother, trying out for the Olympics, has been swimming and diving since he was six years old.

Exercise 95

1. I endorsed the check.
2. We bought a round-trip ticket to Chicago.
3. She went to the front and read.
4. The car I bought last week is blue.
5. Joe is a negligent driver.
6. When he reached his room, Ted started to read a book.
7. I retraced my steps.
8. My sister stood and spoke to the class.
9. We are going to vote for the incumbent candidate.
10. The consensus was radically opposed to having year-round school.
11. The room is 8 by 6 by 10 feet.
12. Gerard Manley Hopkins, author of "God's Grandeur," gives a clear-cut picture of how man is ruining his environment.
13. It is an asset but not a necessity to have a fine camera.
14. Shakespeare's plays have excitement and suspense.
15. Please go over your assignment to eliminate every possible error.

Exercise 96

Answers may vary.

Exercise 97

Answers may vary.

Exercise 98

1. *Madame Bovary*
2. *Frankenstein*
3. *The Brady Bunch*
4. "Our Schools Need Help" *Reader's Digest*
5. *Frasier*
6. *evening*
7. *Richard III*
8. The *s* and *t*
9. *Scholastic Magazine*
10. the *Los Angeles Times*
11. *Mona Lisa*
12. *e g judgment*
13. *Candid Camera*
14. *The Spirit of St. Louis*
15. "Judas"
16. "Cats"
17. "Cats" *Cats*
18. *Robinson Crusoe*
19. *I Love Lucy*
20. *savoir-faire*

Correct Usage Review 1

Part A.

1. A
2. D
3. A
4. A
5. D
6. D
7. C
8. D
9. B
10. A
11. A
12. D
13. D
14. C
15. C
16. A
17. C
18. A
19. C
20. B
21. A
22. B
23. C
24. B
25. B

Part B.

26. If you would have moved the car on time, we would not have received a ticket. *had*
27. This condenser was just installed, therefore, you should check the parts before installing them. *; therefore*
28. Irregardless of what she says, I cannot go at this time. *regardless*
29. Of the two players, Paul is certainly the best. *better*
30. She inferred from John's remarks that you are leaving town. *Correct*

31. There are less items to be checked today. *fewer*

32. She is one of the delegates who was chosen to attend. *were*

33. No one, including Mary and I, have the right to make the decision for him. *me, has*

34. The data that he collected was poor in quality. *were*

35. The reason he lost is because he injured his shoulder. *that*

36. Being that you won the writing contest, you are excused from writing your next paper. *Because*

37. She is a much better player than Tom or me. *I*

38. Working to finish on time, I missed my lunch break. *Correct*

39. I wish that I was able to help him at this time. *were*

40. Sarah is as kind if not kinder than her sister. *as kind as, if not kinder than,*

Correct Usage Review 2

Part A.

1. C	7. D	14. A	21. B
2. E	8. B	15. B	22. D or B
3. B	9. B	16. B	23. C
4. A	10. C	17. D	24. A
5. A	11. C	18. C	25. C
6. D	12. D	19. A	
	13. C	20. C	

Part B.

26. The team was very enthused over its victory against Fillmore. *enthusiastic*

27. Please bring these books there as soon as possible. *take*

28. The climate in California is very healthy. *healthful*

29. Her mumbling aggravated the teacher. *irritated*

30. There was all together too much disturbance at the rally. *altogether*

31. Do you think it will be alright to send the report later? *all right*

32. We were all anxious to attend the football game on Saturday. *eager*

33. It is almost impossible for the President to affect changes in the White House. *effect*

34. It is all ready time to close the gym. *already*

35. Between Mary, Tom, and me, there can never be a strong friendship. *among*

36. If you don't wish to irritate your cold, take plenty of rest. *aggravate*

37. I was completely disinterested in the movie we saw last week. *uninterested*

38. There was alot of packages on the table. *a lot*

39. The building is apt to be unsafe during an earthquake. *likely*

40. All the data collected last week is no longer relevant. *are*

Answers to Unit Tests Level 2

Unit 1—Basic Materials

Part A.

1. L	6. TR	11. TR
2. TR	7. TR	12. L
3. TR	8. L	13. INT
4. INT	9. TR	14. TR
5. L	10. TR	15. TR

Part B.

16. cheering P	20. to leave I	24. gasping P	28. aching A
17. to break I	21. flying G	25. studying P	29. to see I
18. to achieve I	22. knitting G	26. pitching G	30. to watch I
19. filled P	23. hair standing A	27. noticing G	

Part C.

31. B	34. B	37. B	40. A
32. B	35. B	38. A	
33. B	36. B	39. B	

Part D.

41. S	44. O	47. O	50. O
42. O	45. D	48. S	
43. D	46. S	49. D	

Unit 2—Adverb Clauses

Part A.

1. if	6. because	11. if	16. if
2. while	7. even though	12. so that	17. than
3. than	8. if	13. when	18. while
4. if	9. if	14. where	19. when
5. after	10. so that	15. because	20. although

Part B.

Answers may vary.

Part C.

31. A	34. A	37. A	40. B
32. A	35. A	38. A	
33. A	36. A	39. B	

Part D.

41. P	44. P
42. L	45. L
43. L	

Unit 3— Adjective Clauses

Part A.

1. books, magazines—that	11. mother—who
2. books—that	12. boat—that
3. movies—that	13. work—which
4. job—that	14. people—who
4. men, women—who	15. Jane —who
5. Huntington Library—that	16. people—who
7. Bahamas—where	17. jobs—that
8. trip—that	18. John—who
9. house—where	19. news—that
10. Robin Cook—whose	20. show—that

Part B.

21. R	26. R	31. R	36. R
22. R	27. N	32. R	37. R
23. R	28. N	33. N	38. N
24. N	29. N	34. R	39. R
25. N	30. R	35. R	40. N

Unit 4— Noun Clauses

Part A.

1. S	8. S	15. OP	22. S
2. DO	9. S	16. S	23. A
3. DO	10. DO	17. SC	24. DO
4. OP	11. A	18. A	25. DO
5. SC	12. IO	19. DO	
6. OP	13. A	20. DO	
7. OP	14. DO	21. OP	

Part B.

26. A
27. B
28. A
29. A
30. B
31. A
32. B
33. B
34. A
35. A

Part C.

36. Tom asked, "Where did you put my sweater?"
37. "Everyone who comes early," the teacher said, "will have the best seats."
38. Have you read the one-act play "Trifles"?
39. "Where are the basketballs?" the coach yelled.
40. "I think it has vanished," I said.

Unit 5—Compound Sentences

Part A.

1. CX
2. CX
3. CD
4. CD
5. CC
6. S
7. CC
8. CC
9. S
10. CD
11. CD
12. CX
13. S
14. CC
15. CX
16. CD
17. CD
18. CD
19. S
20. CX

Part B.

21. Lois, Jane—neither nor
22. brother, sister—whether or
23. take, do—either or
24. student, athlete—not only but also
25. stupid, wise—either or
26. car, television—neither, nor
27. parents, sister—both and
28. does, will receive—either or
29. Tom, Barbara—whether or
30. attitude, record—neither nor

Part C.

31. If you intend to send the card *tomorrow,* let me sign it first.
32. Her attitude in class caused *problems; consequently,* she had to leave.
33. Jack wants to go to *Hawaii; Mary,* to *Alaska;* and *Joe,* to Cuba.
34. My *watch,* which is very *valuable, was* stolen last night.
35. Last night there was a severe *storm;* the airport was closed until morning.
36. His speech had many good *points,* but it also caused controversy.
37. We knew that Joe was not ready for the *Olympics; however,* he was determined to go.
38. *Marilyn, who* is a great volleyball *player, received* a scholarship to Cal Poly.
39. Buy the *necklace;* it is a great bargain.
40. I work at *Ralph's; in addition,* I write articles for the school paper.
41. I did not want to *cook; moreover,* we had no food in the house.
42. The race was long and *tedious; however,* we won.
43. The earthquake struck at 11:00 *P.M.,* but no one was hurt.
44. She missed the bus for *school; therefore,* she had to walk.
45. My car broke *down; consequently,* my father had to come after me.

Unit 6—Mood, Potential, Parallelism, Transitions

Part A.

1. B	5. A	9. A	13. A
2. B	6. A	10. B	14. A
3. B	7. A	11. B	15. A
4. B	8. A	12. A	

Part B.

16. classmates from your school
17. but that I sing off key
18. into our house
19. and took his daughter to school
20. than because I have never been
21. is not only a strong student, but also a strong leader
22. we could hear loud cheering
23. but the editor turned it down
24. nor basketball
25. but the juniors did not appreciate it
26. but her classmates laughed at it
27. is as good as mine, if not better
    or
    is as good as, if not better than,
28. than going to dances
29. and enjoy the rides
30. my sister likes writing a story

Part C.

31. I	35. I	39. I	43. C
32. C	36. C	40. I	44. I
33. I	37. I	41. C	45. I
34. C	38. I	42. I	

Level 2—Final Examination

Part A.

1. A
2. C
3. B
4. A
5. B

Part B.

6. A	13. B	20. A	27. B
7. A	14. B	21. B	28. A
8. B	15. A	22. A	29. B
9. A	16. A	23. B	30. A
10. B	17. A	24. A	
11. A	18. A	25. B	
12. A	19. B	26. B	

About the Manuscript

Grammar Mastery for Better Writing provides a sequential teaching method with extensive reinforcement exercises developed and piloted by Mary Louise Wanamaker during her career as a high school English teacher. "Both books are designed to help students acquire a better understanding of the English language as it relates to writing," she explains. "The study of grammar is not an end in itself; it is only practical when students understand its importance as a background in their writing development."

Her workbooks were piloted in St. Bonaventure High School in Ventura, California and La Reina High School in Thousand Oaks, California. The teachers at both schools agree with Wanamaker that not only do the students learn the concepts of grammar, but also the teachers themselves master the subject after using her workbooks. Students in the piloting classes have gone on to score higher on achievement tests and do better in college English classes than students who did not have grammar presented to them in a logical way with many drills, reviews, and reinforcements.

> I have been teaching from Wanamaker's materials for the past six years and have witnessed a better understanding of grammar in my students because of the clarity and exercise format of the workbooks. Students seem to grasp grammatical concepts more readily than they ever have before and apply them to their own writing endeavors. . . . As head of our English department, I have witnessed good results from colleagues who have also utilized her materials.
>
> —Jeannette Longwill, English Department Chairperson,
> St. Bonaventure High School, Ventura, California

> Rote memorization of grammar rules may allow someone to do well on an exam or a standardized test, but a true understanding of grammar will allow one to excel in these situations as well as in writing and in appreciating the writing of others. These are the skills [Wanamaker] offered in [her] course and they are skills that I will use for the rest of my life. . . . Because the approach [Wanamaker] took to teaching grammar emphasized the understanding of concepts presented in a logical fashion, I was able to recall and apply the rules of grammar appropriately—even years after my classes with [her] had ended.
>
> —Veronica Garg, former student

> [Wanamaker's] grammar course helped to give me confidence when writing numerous performance reports, awards, and decorations. Although you never get a grade in real life, the use of grammar will directly reflect upon the professionalism of your writing. People will take you more seriously if you write well.
>
> —Mike Fowler, former student

> My writing improved through [Wanamaker's] focus on grammar. I was able to devise a proper sentence, paragraph, and paper, because I knew the rules which govern our language. Knowledge of grammar gave me a set of tools to reach for when I needed to express my thoughts.
>
> —Carrie Mapes, former student

Language Arts Series

Advanced Placement

Advanced Placement English 1: Practical Approaches to Literary Analysis
Advanced Placement English 2: In-depth Analysis of Literary Forms
Advanced Placement Poetry
Advanced Placement Short Story
Advanced Placement Writing 1
Advanced Placement Writing 2

Composition

Advanced Composition (Teacher Manual and Student Workbook)
Basic Composition (Teacher Manual and Student Workbook)
Creative Writing
Daily Writing Topics
Grammar Mastery—For Better Writing (Teacher Guide and Student Workbooks)
Grammar Power—the Essential Elements (Teacher Guide and Student Workbook)
Journalism: Writing for Publication
Research 1: Information Literacy
Research 2: The Research Paper
Writing 1: Learning the Process
Writing 2: Becoming a Writer
Writing Short Stories
Writing Skills and the Job Search

Cross-Curriculum

Doing My Part: Reflections on Community Service for High School Students (Teacher Manual and Student Reflection Handbook)
Peer Mediation:
Training Students in Conflict Resolution
The Positive Teacher: Daily Reflections
Searching for Yourself
Supervisor/Student Teacher Manual
Valuing Others

Literary Forms

Mythology
Nonfiction: A Critical Approach
Participating in the Poem
Science Fiction—19th Century
Short Poems: Their Vitality and Versatility
The Short Story
Thematic Approaches to British Poetry

Literary Traditions

American Literature 1: Beginnings through Civil War
American Literature 2: Civil War to Present
Archetypes in Life, Literature, and Myth
British Literature 1: Beginnings to Age of Reason
British Literature 2: Romantics to the Present
Honors American Literature 1: Beginnings through Nineteenth Century
Honors American Literature 2: World War I to the Present
Multicultural Literature: Essays, Fiction, and Poetry
World Literature 1: A Thematic Approach
World Literature 2: A Thematic Approach

Special Topics

Creative Dramatics in the Classroom
Junior High Language Arts
Let's Read! Young Adult Fiction:
Tools for Individualized Reading Programs, Volumes 1 and 2
Let's Read! Classics and Literary Novels:
Tools for Individualized Reading Programs, Volumes 3 and 4
Reading Strategies
Reading Thematically: History Stories
Speech
Thinking, Reading, Writing, Speaking

The Publisher

All instructional materials identified by the TAP® (Teachers/Authors/Publishers) trademark are developed by a national network of 460 teacher-authors, whose collective educational experience distinguishes the publishing objective of The Center for Learning, a nonprofit educational corporation founded in 1970.

Concentrating on values-related disciplines, the Center publishes humanities and religion curriculum units for use in public and private schools and other educational settings. Approximately 600 language arts, social studies, novel/drama, life issues, and faith publications are available.

Publications are regularly evaluated and updated to meet the changing and diverse needs of teachers and students. Teachers may offer suggestions for development of new publications or revisions of existing titles by contacting

The Center for Learning
Administration/Creative Development
P.O. Box 417, Evergreen Road
Villa Maria, PA 16155
(800) 767-9090 • FAX (724) 964-1802

The Center for Learning
Editorial/Prepress
24600 Detroit Road, Suite 201
Westlake, OH 44145
(440) 250-9341 • FAX (440) 250-9715

For a free catalog containing order and price information and a descriptive listing of titles, contact

The Center for Learning
Customer Service
P.O. Box 910, Evergreen Road
Villa Maria, PA 16155
(724) 964-8083 • (800) 767-9090
FAX (888) 767-8080
http://www.centerforlearning.org